GET EB2/NIW
Green Card from Abroad With Low Budget

Chien Min Kuo

Copyright © 2021 by ScholarWorld Inc.

All rights reserved. This book or any portion thereof may not be reproduced or used in any manner whatsoever without the express written permission of the publisher except for the use of brief quotations in a book review.

The characters and events portrayed in this book are fictitious. Any similarity to real persons, living or dead, is coincidental and not intended by the author.

No part of this book may be reproduced, or stored in a retrieval system, or transmitted in any form or by any means, electronic, mechanical, photocopying, recording, or otherwise, without express written permission of the publisher.

First Printing, 2021

Cover design by: Art Painter

Author Biography

Kuo Chien Min was born in Taiwan and became a permanent resident of the U.S.A. in 2020. He is a Christian. He holds B.S., M.S., and Ph.D. degrees in Information Management from Taiwan. He has served as a second lieutenant, programmer, assistant researcher, assistant professor, associate professor, author, and inventor. He has published 22 peer-reviewed articles in leading journals, including Information Sciences (SCI), Program (SSCI), The Electronic Library (SSCI), and others. Additionally, he has 45 articles published in academic conference proceedings. He also owns over 350 patents in Taiwan, China, and the USA. He has authored several books, such as "The Analysis and Introduction of English Core Journal and Thesis Between 1998 to 2008," "Apply Biology to Business Administration," "Learn the Biology Wisdom from the Holy Bible," and more.

Preface

In this book, I aim to share my personal experiences on how to obtain the EB2/NIW green card for the United States on a limited budget. This visa category is designed for individuals who are members of professions requiring advanced degrees or those with exceptional abilities, including requests for national interest waivers. Unlike many other visa categories, the EB2/NIW does not require a U.S. employer as a sponsor.

Since I had limited funds for my application, I sought to minimize costs and navigate the process efficiently. While it is possible to complete the process entirely on your own (DIY), I recommend consulting a professional immigration lawyer during the early stages. This is especially important when preparing the I-140 petition, as it can be challenging to handle without prior experience.

Before applying for my green card, I had never studied, lived, or worked in the United States. I applied for the green card from abroad, making my journey unique. In this book, I share numerous experiences and resources to guide you through the process.

Throughout my application, I prepared all documents and materials meticulously, often double-checking details online to ensure accuracy. Most importantly, I believe that God's blessings enabled me to succeed in every step of the process without any rejections or RFEs (Requests for Evidence).

I hope my experiences can provide valuable insights and guidance for your journey. May God bless you, and best of luck! Best wishes,

Chien Min Kuo, January 15, 2021

Table of Content

Copyright

Author Biography

Preface

1. Workflow Introduction

2. Seek Lawyer with Limited Budget

3. Pay and Save the Fees

4. Reference Letter

5. Petition Letter

6. Exhibit for Supporting Documents

7. File the Case

8. Submit DS-260

9. Health Exam

10. Interview

11. Get the Green Card

Appendix

CHAPTER I. WORKFLOW INTRODUCTION

There are thirty steps illustrated in Figure 1-1. The details of these steps will be described in the following ten chapters. For a brief description, they are as follows:

1) Prepare the CV

Firstly, the applicant should prepare a personal curriculum vitae (CV) before contacting a lawyer. If you don't prepare it, the immigration lawyer will require you to provide this to evaluate your case. Therefore, the applicant should prepare this file as the first step.

2) Prepare the Google Scholar Profile

You can currently generate your personal Google Scholar profile at [Google Scholar](http://scholar.google.com). It includes citation counts and an h-index for your academic publications. Generally, the lawyer will evaluate your case based on this to determine if they will provide you with an "approval or refund" solution.

3) Seek a Suitable Lawyer

Many immigration lawyers can be found on the internet. Some will display their case pass rates on their websites. Generally, it is more expensive to find a local lawyer or immigration company in your own country. It will be cheaper to look for a lawyer located in the United States.

4) Prepare Valid Passport and Photo

Applicants need to fill out many forms in the future, requiring a valid passport. If the passports of you and your family members are set to expire within six months, please renew them. You will also need a new photo taken within the last six months. If your case is reviewed by USCIS for more than six months, you will need to take a new picture after you get approved by USCIS.

5) Decide the Visa Category

The lawyer will decide the suitable visa category for you after evaluating your CV and Google Scholar profile. They will determine whether they will provide the "approval or refund" solution for you.

6) Decide Recommender List

Six recommendation letters will be needed when you submit your case. Applicants need to prepare a potential recommender list early. Not all potential recommenders will agree to help you, so you should list more than six potential recommenders.

7) Draft Reference Letters

If you seek help from an immigration lawyer, they will draft the reference letters for you. All you need to do is provide them with your achievements and the recommenders' CVs.

8) Recommenders Modify and Sign Letter

After reviewing the six draft reference letters, you can send them to the recommenders. Once they review and modify the letters, you can ask them to sign their names and then mail them back to you by email or physical mail.

9) Lawyer Draft Petition Letter

This is the most important part of the whole procedure. Generally, a professional immigration lawyer will help you with this. If you try to do this yourself, it is better to get many examples, although it is not easy to find samples on the internet.

10) Revise and Print the Petition Letter

Review and revise the petition letter before you confirm it. Once confirmed, you can print it or notify the lawyer's assistant to print it.

11) Prepare Supporting Documents

You will need to prepare lots of supporting documents, which I will list in Chapter Six. It will take you at least two months to prepare these documents.

12) Mail Supporting Documents to Lawyer

After collecting all the supporting documents, applicants will need a box to mail them to the lawyer.

13) Organize Exhibits

The lawyer will organize exhibits obtained from the applicant and prepare to file the case within one week.

14) Fill out the Form G-28

Form G-28 is the notice of entry of appearance as an attorney or accredited representative. Use this form to provide information about your eligibility to act on behalf of an applicant, petitioner, or respondent.

15) Fill out the Form ETA-750

Applicants abroad need to fill out the form ETA-750-Part B, the application for alien employment certification. Examples will be provided in Chapter Seven.

16) Fill out the Form I-140

Use this form to petition for an alien worker to become a permanent resident in the United States. This is the most important form and requires a professional petition letter.

17) Pay the Fee

You will need to pay USCIS several times. If you get the approval or refund from the immigration lawyer, you just need to pay them once. Some applicants and cases need to pay the lawyer multiple times, depending on the contract between the applicant and lawyer.

18) File the Case

Before submitting your case, it will take you almost four to twelve months to prepare all the materials. Prepare everything carefully to avoid getting a Request for Evidence (RFE) from USCIS in the future.

19) Receive the Receipt from USCIS

After filing the case, you will get two receipts confirming you have paid the fee and submitted the case successfully. In the future, you can inquire about your case status using the receipt number and received date.

20) Wait Several Months

Generally, applicants have to wait at least six months. I waited for eight months. Some special cases were approved within 30 days or 180 days.

21) RFE or Not

Some cases will receive an RFE (Request for Evidence), a written request for more information and documentation that USCIS mails out if they believe they don't have enough evidence to approve or deny a given application.

22) Get Form I-797C (Notice of Action)

If your case is approved, you will get a mail with Form I-797C, notifying you that your petition was approved.

23) Prepare and Submit Form DS-260

Applicants applying for a green card from outside the U.S. need to file the DS-260 online form, handled through the National Visa Center (NVC) and your local U.S. embassy or consulate.

24) Medical Examination

Before being scheduled for an interview, the applicant and their family members should go to a hospital assigned by your local U.S. embassy or consulate for a medical examination.

25) Interview

The Visa bulletin summarizes the availability of immigrant numbers. USCIS will schedule an interview if your category status becomes current. Most countries do not need to wait long, but applicants from China and India generally have to wait many years.

26) Get the Yellow Package

If you are approved in the interview, you will receive a yellow package and your passport with a visa. You must bring them to the U.S. within six months after the interview.

27) Apply for the Green Card Online

After your case is approved, you can apply for the green card online. You should have a U.S. address. It is okay to use a friend's address, but their name must be on your application.

28) Pay the Fee

You can pay the fee to make your green card at the following website: [USCIS Immigrant Fee](https://my.uscis.gov/uscis-immigrant-fee). After paying, you can trace the status. You should wait one to four months to get the green cards.

29) Travel to the USA

You must travel to the U.S. within six months after the interview. If it expires, you will need another medical examination. You can also choose to delay by returning the yellow package to the embassy or consulate, triggering another interview appointment.

30) Get the Green Card

The green card will be delivered to your provided address after border officials take away your yellow package, usually within one to four months. Before receiving the green card, you can use your passport with the visa to apply for a social security card or bank account. The passport with the border entry seal will be valid for one year.

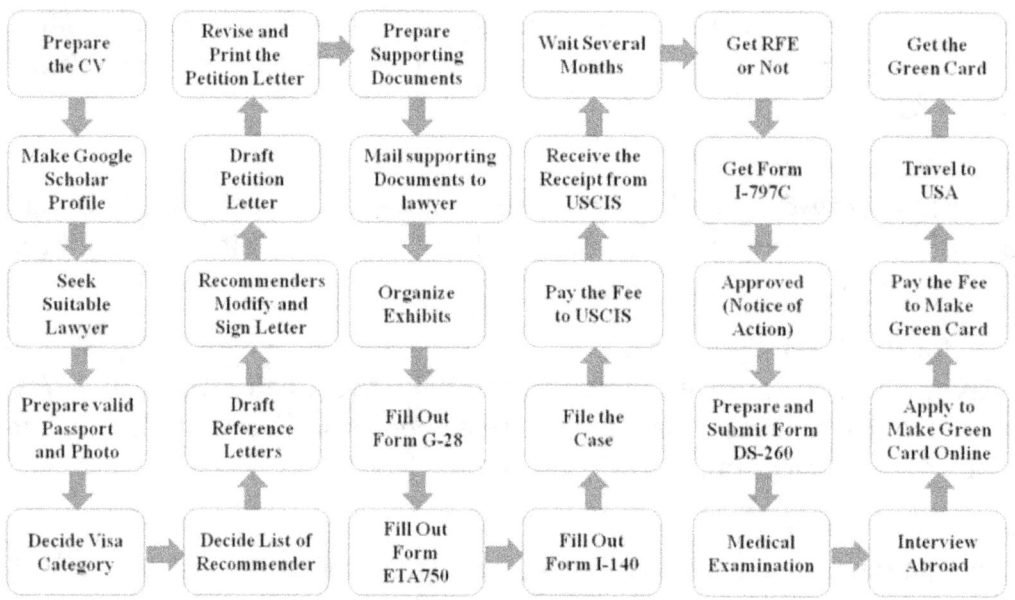

Figure 1-1 The Workflow of NIW/EB2 Case

CHAPTER II. SEEK LAWYER WITH LIMITED BUDGET

First, you should prepare your personal CV and Google Scholar or Google Patent profile. Please refer to Figures 2-1 and 2-2. You can find many lawyers on the internet. In general, it is cheaper to seek help from a lawyer in the U.S.A. than from a domestic immigration company. Many lawyers in the U.S.A. also provide customer services in different languages. Therefore, I recommend that applicants seek help from a lawyer abroad. In my case, I only paid five thousand dollars to a lawyer before I got the green card. I previously sought help from immigration companies, but it would have cost me about sixty thousand dollars if I had asked them to help me apply for the green card. There is a large gap between these costs.

They will provide an online system to let you upload documents, which they will review and comment on. They also offer free phone calls in your native language. However, I went through almost the entire procedure using the online system instead of phone calls.

You will need to decide on the right category suitable for you. A lawyer will evaluate your case and give you suggestions. However, it would cost you more money if you apply for two categories (e.g., EB1, NIW) at the same time. This approach can increase your approval rate and decrease the turnaround time. If you have a larger budget, you may consider this option. If your budget is limited, choose the most suitable category for your case.

In addition, you must prepare a passport that is valid for more than one year before it expires. If you have multiple names, you will need to use only the one listed on the passport.

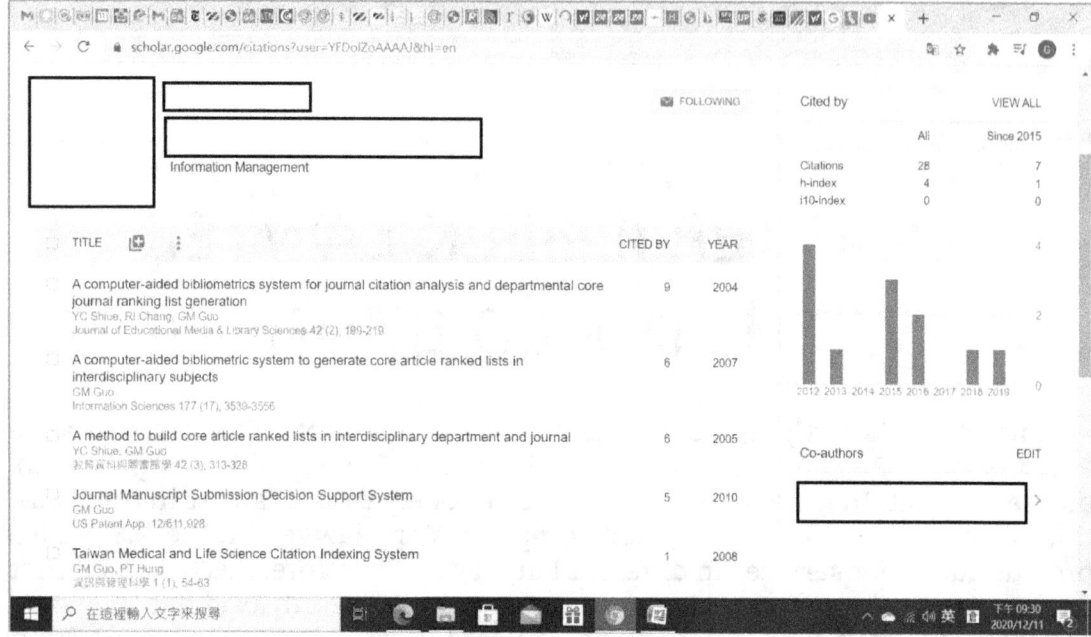

Figure 2-1 Google Scholar Profile Example

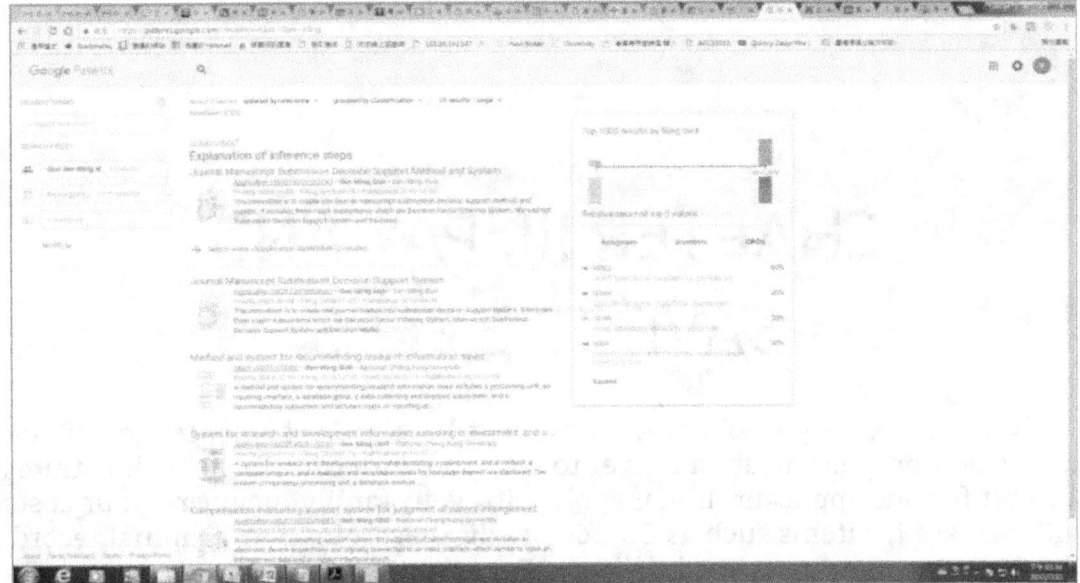

Figure 2-2 Google Patent Profile Example

CHAPTER III. PAY AND SAVE THE FEES

If you want to pay DS-260 fees, you must have a U.S. bank account. If you don't have one, you can ask a lawyer to help you with this. Table 3-1 illustrates the cost for one applicant. If you apply with your family members, your costs will increase for items such as DS-260, medical examination, criminal record, visa delivery, and green card delivery. For example, there are five people in my family. The total cost increased to about twelve thousand dollars, which is double the cost for one person. In Table 3-1, you should pay money to five entities: 1) Government, 2) Lawyer, 3) Hospital, 4) Logistic Company, and 5) Credential Evaluation Company.

The cheapest way to apply for a green card is to do it yourself (DIY). However, it is difficult to prepare the I-140 by yourself. Therefore, you can seek a lawyer to help you with the I-140. After it is approved, you can try to DIY the rest to save money. I try to limit my budget as much as possible. If you apply with your family members, you can save more money. For example, filing an I-140 would cost you 700 dollars, but it would only need $345*5 for five people in one case.

Table 3-1 The Fees Table

Item	Fee
Lawyer Fee For I-140	$5,000
Credential Evaluation and Authentication Report Of Your Diploma	$107
File I-140 (EB-1A, EB-1B, EB-2 NIW)	$700
DS-260 Interview and Final Fee	$220
Medical Examination Fee	$200
Vaccine For MMR Or Others	$200
Criminal Record in U.K.	$75
Criminal Record in Taiwan	$3
Visa Delivery	$10
Make Green Card And Delivery	$220
Sum	$6,735

Do not apply for any premium services such as criminal record checks, credential evaluations, and so on. These will cost you more money compared to using the standard services. For example, the criminal record fee for premium service in the U.K. is £95, and it takes 4 working days to process (excluding Saturday, Sunday, and U.K. bank holidays). The standard service costs £55 and takes 12 working days to process.

Additionally, children do not need vaccination fees, but adults need the MMR vaccine, which would cost around $100 to $200. Here are the details:

- **Standard service**: £55 - 12 working days to process (excluding Saturday, Sunday, and U.K. bank holidays).
- **Premium service**: £95 - 4 working days to process (excluding Saturday, Sunday, and U.K. bank holidays).

Don't forget to pay the fee for your green card after your interview. If you pay $220 by credit card, you can receive the green card two or three months after landing in the United States.

There is one fee calculator on the internet (Figure 3-1). You can access it at the following website. https://www.uscis.gov/feecalculator

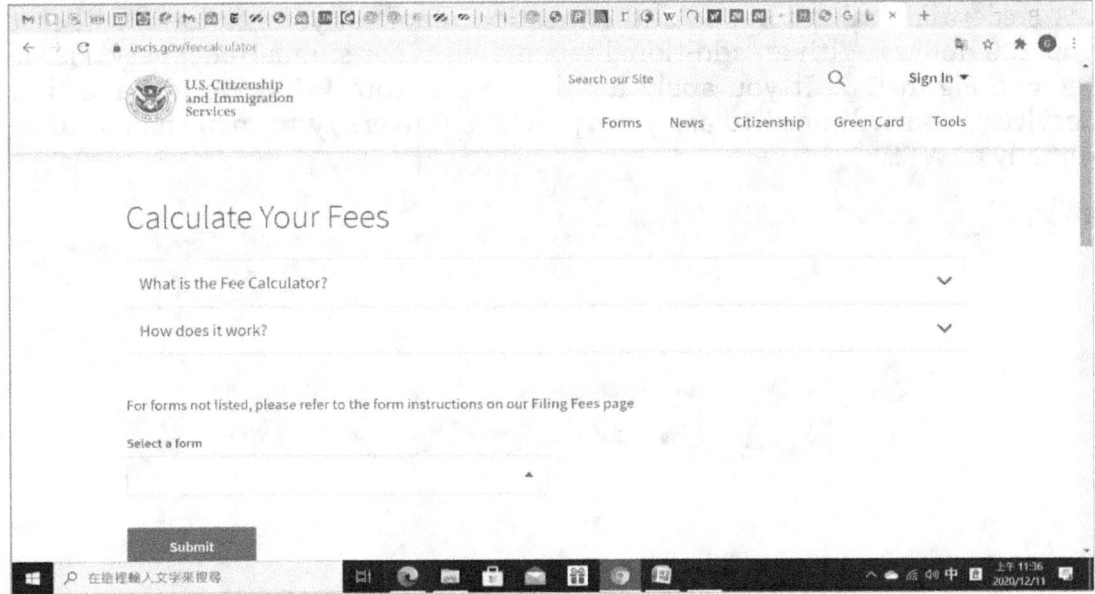

Figure 3-1 The Fee Calculator

A credential evaluation and authentication report of your diploma will cost you 100 dollars, with an additional seven dollars for standard delivery. Please refer to Figure 3-2. If you apply for the report from WES (World Education Services), you will need to ask your previous university to mail the envelope directly to WES.

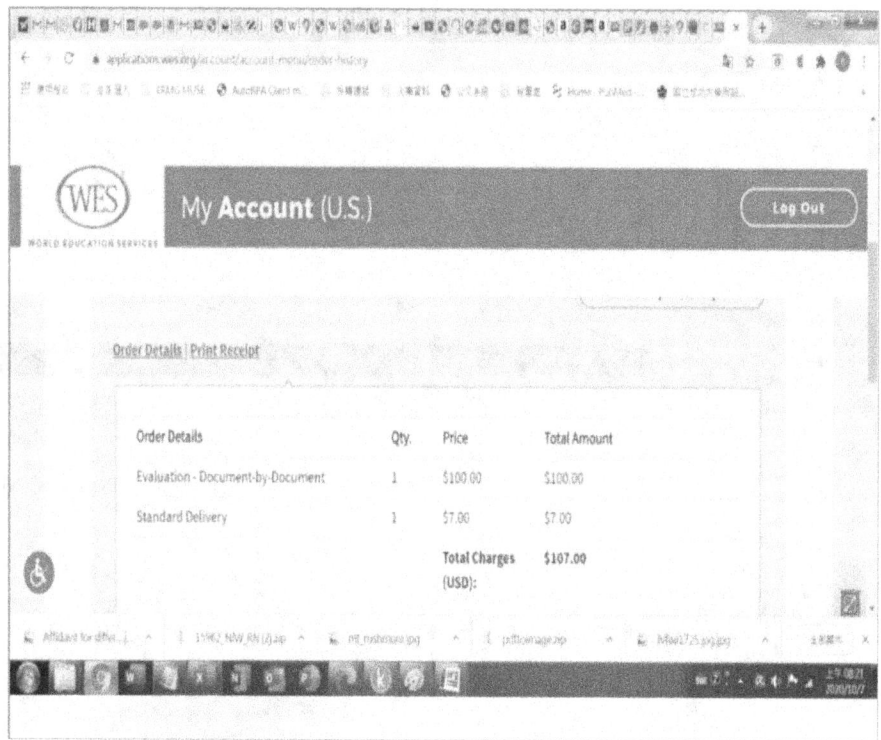

Figure 3-2 Authentication Report Fee of Diploma.

CHAPTER IV. REFERENCE LETTER

You will need six reference letters, including dependent and independent references. For the independent references, you may receive rejected responses easily. Even people who have cited your paper before might decline your invitations. You might try asking individuals whose papers you have reviewed and accepted for publication in the past. You should provide not only six reference letters but also their CVs.

Two reference letter examples are provided below. Please check them as follows:

1) Dependent Reference Letter Example

[Please insert date of signature]

To Whom It Concerns,

I have been very impressed by the amount of interest that Dr. Min Chien Kuo's work has generated among professionals in the field, which has aptly reflected its significance to areas of critical importance to the U.S. and the world. Dr. Kuo has consistently produced findings of great worth in the area of information science, as demonstrated by his work being explicitly mentioned in laws covering the process of hospital evaluation issued by the Taiwanese Ministry of Health and Welfare. That Dr. Kuo has been able to produce research received so enthusiastically by the scientific community, government departments, and the private sector is the hallmark of someone who has assumed a true leadership role in his field. I therefore formally recommend Dr. Kuo to this department without hesitation.

Please allow me to briefly summarize my own qualifications, as well as my relationship with Dr. Kuo, before continuing this recommendation. My name is XXX, and I am a Professor in the Department of XXX at National Taiwan University. My research interests lie in the areas of multimedia networking, data mining and machine learning, wireless sensor networks, computer security and database systems, and bioinformatics. I earned my Ph.D. degree at Taiwan's Chiao-Tung University in the area of computer science. My position at National Taiwan University is a research position, which involves preparing work for peer-reviewed publications, and this is how I've come to work with Dr. Kuo. My understanding of the outstanding contributions he has made in his field stems primarily from the fact that we have collaborated on a research paper published in *Journal of XXX*. I also instructed him in the subject of bioinformatics while he attended National Central University.

Providing one indication of Dr. Kuo's reputation in the information science community is his publication and citation record, which shows that his work has been referenced multiple times and presented in highly ranked journals. These facts show that his findings have provided an ideal foundation for other efforts in the field and confirm his influential status as researcher. The demonstrable utility of Dr. Kuo's published research also neatly mirrors the deep import of his work. Because Dr. Kuo's work leads to innovations in information retrieval and aids the efforts of scholars, his work has a powerful impact felt in academia and multiple important industries. Dr. Kuo's research thus constitutes an invaluable asset to national interests.

I would also like to point out that Dr. Kuo has encouraged progress in the scientific community by serving as a peer reviewer for esteemed journals. He has provided his criticism and comments over 10 times on manuscripts submitted to *Program*, *Information and Management Science*, *Information Sciences*, and more. Dr. Kuo's frequent invitations to perform peer review confirm that he is an accomplished researcher in his discipline.

Dr. Kuo's extensive credentials provide a further picture of the abilities he is able to bring to bear on individual research projects. He began his scientific career at Ming Chuan University, located in Taipei, Taiwan, and earned his bachelor's degrees from this institution before earning an M.Sc. at National Pingtung University of Science and Technology. Afterward, Dr. Kuo studied the subject of information management at National Central University to earn his Ph.D. Dr. Kuo is currently working as an Associate Professor at XXX and concurrently works both as a consultant with ScholarWorld Inc. and as an Administrator at the VUE Exam Center, run by Pearson VUE Inc. Dr. Kuo also worked as an Assistant Researcher at Chunghwa Telecom Inc. before taking on his current roles. Such versatile skills and rigorous training as those possessed by Dr. Kuo are only found among the most highly qualified information science researchers, and Dr. Kuo's background has amply provided him with the skills needed to attain his many career achievements.

One such achievement is Dr. Kuo's novel system for evaluating the research performance of journals in Taiwan, called the Taiwan Science Citation Index System. This system leverages bibliometrics, statistics, AI, and text mining techniques to analyze journal performance. To make the system operational, Dr. Kuo created novel metadata formats from source articles and designed new research indices. These include the journal international impact index, journal cheat index, journal subscription recommendation index, and scholar confidence index. Some other capabilities that Dr. Kuo included in his system are generation of classic and original paper designations, classification of the most popular and trending subjects, generation of keywords from field dictionaries, and identification of researchers as award candidates based on objective data. Dr. Kuo was given a research budget from the National Science Foundation and ScholarWorld Corporation to apply his system to the corpus of research in certain scientific fields in Taiwan. The information he has provided supplements existing databases covering social science and art citations in the country. After collecting around 400,000 references and building his database, Dr. Kuo generated Journal Citation Report information for 220 Taiwanese scientific journals. He found that the average impact factor of these journals is 0.18. His work provides a function similar to that provided by Web of Science for English language journals and articles. Many professionals representing journals in Taiwan have already contacted Dr. Kuo to get their journals added to the indexing system he created.

In sum, I believe that Dr. Kuo's remaining in the U.S. information science community is the best choice for the nation. Please feel free to notify me if I can be of further help in this regard.

Yours sincerely,

XXX, Ph.D.

2) Independent Reference Letter Example

[Please insert date of signature]

Dear USCIS Officer,

My name is Dr. XXX. I currently work as Senior Lecturer in XXX. I have previous experience as a Senior Researcher in the Department of Informatics of the XXX University and acted as Director of the department's Analytics and Data Science Program. I earned my PhD at XXX, and I hold an MSc in engineering, with a specialization in information retrieval, from the XXX.

I write now to offer my fullest recommendation of Dr. Chien-Min Kuo, whose information science contributions have proven highly important to researchers across the world. I myself, in fact, have referenced Dr. Kuo's findings in my own work. This fact, along with our shared research interests, prepares me to speak to Dr. Kuo's merits and describe the impact of research projects he has undertaken in his career, even though we have not had the opportunity to collaborate on any professional projects.

Dr. Kuo's research in the field of information has a broad impact, and the need for this work has been recognized by important organizations in the U.S. Chris Belter, a researcher working with the NOAA Central Library, has written that the "use of bibliometrics is increasing rapidly" and has recommended that bibliometrics techniques be used to complement peer review and raise new questions about the state of research in particular areas or within particular fields. Dr. Kuo has conducted significant research toward enhancing the use of bibliometrics-based practices, and his work has also provided new knowledge in the realm of meta-research. Such work is crucial for fully realizing the benefits of bibliometrics in guiding the research of the future and bringing scholarship to greater fruition. Thus, it is easy to say that Dr. Kuo's work represents a sizeable national contribution by any measure.

Dr. Kuo's work on computer-aided bibliometric systems has inspired further research and provided the research community with means to further related efforts. As mentioned above, I have cited research of Dr. Kuo's, which he published in the journal *Information Sciences*, within a co-authored article that my collaborators and I published in the same journal. Our research into developing a novel indexing factor for research journals was informed by Dr. Kuo's computer-aided method for generating core article ranked lists. His work was certainly a helpful resource for our own research on related topics, providing fundamental information that has pushed the field forward. Moreover, our citation is also just a part of the recognition his work has received, amounting to one out of almost 20 accrued through his work so far.

Dr. Kuo's work has also led to multiple publications in a range of internationally circulated journals, which has ensured a wide audience for his efforts in the field. Dr. Kuo's research frequently serves as a guide for other scientists, which confirms his status as an influential member of the information science research community.

At their core, bibliometrics systems are designed to impart useful information about research to their users, and computer-generated versions of these systems make use of technology to provide information in a more efficient and accessible manner than manual solutions. The information provided by Dr. Kuo's new system relates to important, pioneering, and milestone papers. Important papers are among the most highly cited in their category, while pioneering papers provide information about new subject matter, and milestone papers contain breakthrough discoveries that subsequently draw great attention from the field. Dr. Kuo used four proposed indicators, subject total cited counts (STCC), subject reference cited counts (SRCC) subject reference period impact, and subject reference cited history, to generate core article ranked lists in specific academic subjects. Dr. Kuo focused his subsequent research on the subjects of E-commerce, Data Mining, Supply Chain, Image Processing, Enterprise Resource Planning, Microarray, and Expert

Systems. By analyzing the turning point patterns of each subject, Dr. Kuo found that three commonly held myths regarding published research were disproven by the data. The top ten papers in these subjects were not all submitted to Science Citation Index (SCI) journals, over 20% of papers with citation counts above 4 were also not submitted to SCI journals, and not all articles published in top journals were highly cited. This information is useful for individual researchers as well as for institutions, such as libraries, that purchase scientific journals and articles.

Dr. Kuo also possesses a deep background of meaningful academic and professional experience, encompassing work and training at premier institutions. Prior to beginning his current work as an Assistant Professor at the XXX, Dr. Kuo completed his education, earning a BSc at Ming Chuan University and an MSc at National Pingtung University of Science and Technology. Dr. Kuo went on to earn a PhD from the National Central University. Dr. Kuo has focused his studies on the area of information science, and this has served him in positions as an Assistant Researcher at Chunghwa Telecom Inc. and Administrator at the VUE Exam Center in Taiwan, a position he still holds today. He has also been working as a Senior Technology Consultant for ScholarWorld Inc. since 2007. Dr. Kuo's career has also included service to the field as a peer referee, in which capacity he has reviewed manuscripts for *Information Sciences, Computers and Electrical Engineering*, and more. Dr. Kuo's academic and professional background provides further perspective on Dr. Kuo's place as a leading researcher in his field.

Indeed, combined with the high number of research accomplishments he has seen in his work, Dr. Kuo's experience and aptitude have earned him the distinction of being one of the most advanced individuals currently working in his areas of expertise today. It is thus my strong belief that scientific interests of the U.S. would be best served by retaining Dr. Kuo in the domestic research community.

Respectfully yours,

XXX PhD

CHAPTER V. PETITION LETTER

The petition letter is very important and requires evidence to support it. Some examples are provided in the following sections:

1) Petition Letter Example

Date: XX/XX/2018

To: USCIS
Attn: I-140
P.O. Box 660128
Dallas, TX 75266

RE: Immigrant Petition for Alien Worker

  Petitioner/Beneficiary: Min Chien Kuo, Ph.D.

  Type of Petition: I-140

  Classification Sought: INA §203(b)(2)(B)
             National Interest Waiver

  This letter is respectfully submitted in support of Dr. Min Chien Kuo's immigrant petition for classification as a member of the professions holding an advanced degree requesting a national interest waiver of the requirement of a job offer. The submitted evidence demonstrates that Dr. Kuo qualifies for a national interest waiver under the analytical framework set forth in *Matter of DHANASAR*, 26 I&N Dec. 884 (AAO 2016). Specifically, the submitted evidence will prove:

  a. Dr. Kuo is a member of the professions holding an advanced degree

  b. Dr. Kuo's proposed endeavor has both substantial merit and national importance;

  c. Dr. Kuo is well positioned to advance the proposed endeavor; and

  d. On balance, it would be beneficial to the United States to waive the requirements of a job offer and thus of a labor certification.

I.   **Dr. Kuo is a member of the professions holding an advanced degree**

Dr. Kuo received a Ph.D. from XX University in 200X. As evidence of this, we are submitting copies of Dr. Kuo's diploma and transcripts (Exhibit [advanced degree, transcripts]).Since Dr. Kuo completed his education outside the United States, we are also submitting a detailed advisory evaluation of his educational credentials (Exhibit [degree evaluation]).Based on his education and experience, Dr. Kuo intends to continue to pursue work in information science, focusing on XX systems by extending his research on XX methodology (Exhibit [personal statement]). As such, Dr. Kuo is qualified as a member of the professions holding an advanced degree.

II. **Dr. Kuo's proposed endeavor has both substantial merit and national importance**

As an expert in the field of information science, Dr. Kuo proposes to continue his researchon XX systems. As evidence of this, we are submitting evidence of his future plans(Exhibit[personal statement]).Research in this area is of great importance because it **provides improved tools for research professionals, who increasingly need access to high quality databases. According to the UK digital solutions company Jisc, "Using search engines effectively is now a key skill for researchers, but more could be done to equip...researchers with the tools they need"** (Exhibit[Jisc page on search engines for researchers]).Having developed a number of critical tools, Dr. Kuo has made significant gains towards this end. Dr. Kuo's proposed research therefore has substantial merit. Fellow experts in the field provide additional insight into the merit of this endeavor:

- *"Dr. Kuo's research has taken place in areas of deep national and international concern. As researchers working for Jisc, a firm in the United Kingdom engaged in the education and research field, describe, using search engines effectively is now a key skill for researchers worldwide. Dr. Kuo's methods for indexing research trends and forecasting popular research topics is suitable for use with journal search engines, as well as patent, news, and general search engines. Providing and improving tools of this nature is a matter of interest for both private and public center entities, and Dr. Kuo's research in particular directly ties into the goal of making access to information more efficient and effective. His work in this area has exhibited great scientific value and provides clear and direct benefit to U.S. and global interests."*(Exhibit 2. Dr. XX, Professor Emeritus, Dietrich College of Social Sciences, XX University, Country)

- *"Dr. Kuo has conducted significant research toward enhancing the use of bibliometric-based practices, and his work has also provided new knowledge in the realm of meta-research. Such work is crucial for fully realizing the benefits of bibliometrics in guiding the research of the future and bringing scholarship to greater fruition. Thus, it is easy to say that Dr. Kuo's work represents a sizeable national contribution by any measure."*(Exhibit 4. Dr. XX, Senior Lecturer in Business Analytics, XX Business School, University of XX) (**Independent Advisory Opinion**)

Dr. Kuo's proposed endeavor also has broad implications for the field. **Dr. Kuo's work significantly impacts the advancement and use of new technology in the United States. This is a major concern in the country because of the widespread impact that computer and internet technology has on the nation. In fact, according to the Pew Research Center, 88% of Americans use the internet for business and personal reasons** (Exhibit Pew Research Center page on American technology use). Dr. Kuo's proposed research is therefore also nationally important. Fellow experts in the field have provided further detail on the importance of this endeavor to the

United States:

- "Strong reception of these findings should come as no surprise, considering that his work has addressed issues of deep national concern. According to Pew Research Center polls on internet and technology use in the United States, around 77% of Americans currently own Smart phones, up from 35% in the year 2011, Global sales of smart phones also grew 3.9% year of year in the first quarter of 2016, with many developing markets such as India representing areas of untapped growth for the future. Research on architectural innovations and new applications for Smart phones is necessary for keeping these technologies in a position to provide economic benefits for the country, which relies heavily on the tech sector for economic strength. Dr. Kuo's research has equipped researchers with new knowledge of this very nature, making his research germane to national interests and those of the scientific profession. The degree of success that Dr. Kuo has attained in this work has positioned him at the very forefront of his field, which, in today's landscape, is fast-paced, critical, and highly competitive."(Exhibit 3. Mr. XX Chen, Database Administrator, XX University) (**Independent Advisory Opinion**)

- "Dr. Kuo is a researcher who has uniquely aided progress in his area of expertise, which pertains to use of information science to advance the areas of bibliometrics and technology. His research in this area has yielded new methods and systems for improving products such as the talking pen used to educate many children and adolescents in East Asia. The economic importance of Dr. Kuo's work in technology is profound in a country like the United States, which has an economy driven by the growth and job opportunities Created by the needs of technology consumers. The U.S. industry organization CompTIA has found that the technology sector accounted for 7.1% of the country's overall GDP and 11.6% of its private sector payroll in 2016. The tech industry also employed 6.9 million American workers during that year. Dr. Kuo's work has broken important new ground in his work and research with smartphones, other technologies like the talking pen, and with bibliometrics software that represents a new frontier in the analysis of research taking place today. As such, Dr. Kuo's studies are deeply valuable to research aims in his field and assist in intrinsically important efforts toward providing the world community with superior technological products and devices."(Exhibit 5. Mr. XX Lin, Chief Executive Officer, XX Corporation) (**Independent Advisory Opinion**)

Because Dr. Kuo's proposed endeavor has both substantial merit and national importance, he satisfies this prong.

III.   **Dr. Kuo is well positioned to advance the proposed endeavor**

Dr. Kuo's education, experience, and expertise in his field have well positioned him to advance the proposed endeavor. Dr. Kuo received his B.Sc. at XX University and then attended XX University for his M.Sc. He finished his Ph.D. at XX University before becoming an assistant professor at XX University (Exhibits [degrees, CV]). Based on this history in the field, Dr. Kuo intends to pursue research related to computer-aided bibliometric systems, particularly the advancement of bibliometric systems and technology (Exhibit [personal statement]). Experts in the field discuss his background and skill set:

- "Dr. Kuo's extensive credentials provide a further picture of the abilities he is able to bring to bear on individual research projects. He began his scientific career at XX University, located in Taipei, Taiwan, and earned his bachelor's degrees from this institution before earning an M.Sc. at XX University. Afterward, Dr. Kuo studied the subject of information management at XX University to earn his Ph.D. Dr. Kuo is currently working as an Assistant Professor XX University and concurrently works both as a consultant with ScholarWorld Inc, and as an Administrator at the VUE Exam Center, run by Pearson VUE Inc. Dr. Kuo also worked as an Assistant Researcher at Chunghwa Telecom Inc. before taking on his current roles. Such versatile skills and rigorous training as those possessed by Dr. Kuo are only found among the most highly qualified information science researchers, and Dr. Kuo's background has amply provided him with the skills needed to attain his many career achievements."(Exhibit 1. Dr. XX, Professor, Department of XX, XX University)

- "Dr. Kuo also possesses a deep background of meaningful academic and professional experience, encompassing work and training at premier institutions. Prior to beginning his current work as an Assistant Professor at the XX University, Dr. Kuo completed his education, earning a BSc at XX University and an MSc at XX University. Dr. Kuo went on to earn a PhD from the XX University. Dr. Kuo has focused his studies on the area of information science, and this has served him in positions as an Assistant Researcher at Chunghwa Telecom Inc. and Administrator at the VUE Exam Center in Taiwan, a position he still holds today. He has also been working as a Senior Technology Consultant for ScholarWorld Inc. since 2007. Dr. Kuo's career has also included service to the field as a peer referee, in which capacity he has reviewed manuscripts for Information Sciences, Computers and Electrical Engineering, and more. Dr. Kuo's academic and professional background provides further perspective on Dr. Kuo's place as a leading researcher in his field. Indeed, combined with the high number of research accomplishments he has seen in his work, Dr. Kuo's experience and aptitude have earned him the distinction of being one of the most advanced individuals currently working in his areas of expertise today. It is thus my strong belief that scientific interests of the U.S. would be best served by retaining Dr. Kuo in the domestic research community."(Exhibit 4. Dr. XX, Senior Lecturer in Business Analytics, XX Business School, University of XX) (**Independent Advisory Opinion**)

Throughout his time working in the field, Dr. Kuo has also built an impressive record of publication. As evidence of his contributions, Dr. Kuo's work has resulted in **64 peer-reviewed articles, 2 books, 1 U.S. patent, 1 U.S. patent application, 1 Chinese patent, and 363 Taiwanese patents** (Exhibits[publications, U.S. patent, U.S. patent application, Chinese patent, Taiwanese patents]). Moreover, these papers have been published in one of the top journals in Dr. Kuo's field, which reflects his peers' recognition of the value of this research. For example, *InformationSciences* has an **Impact Factor of 4.832 and is ranked #5** in Engineering and Computer Science (general) by Google Scholar (Exhibits [publications, journal rankings]).

Experts in the field confirm how Dr. Kuo's record of successful research has well positioned him to continue advancing the endeavor:

- "Also confirming Dr. Kuo's important standing in the research community is the publication of his work in such journals as Information Sciences, one of the

> top outlets in the field. The international circulation of his work ensures that researcher worldwide have been provided valuable information to support their own inquiries. Dr. Kuo has also played an important role in reviewing the work of other researchers. Respected journals such as the Eurasia Journal of Mathematics, Science and Technology Education, Information Sciences, and more have called upon Dr. Kuo to perform peer review duties. The eminent commercial relevance of Dr. Kuo's work is also indicated by the 300-plus Taiwanese, China and USA patents he has been granted for his research. These are not accomplishments that many researchers are able to achieve, and it is thus no exaggeration to say that Dr. Kuo's contributions have elevated him above the majority of his peers."(Exhibit 2. Dr. XX, Professor Emeritus, Dietrich College of Social Sciences, XX University, Country)

> "His research to date has already led to numerous peer-reviewed publications and an astonishing 351 Taiwanese patents. His articles have also appeared in a range of top-flight journals such as Information Science, a fact that neatly underlines the consistent rigor his research has demonstrated. As someone working in areas related to Dr. Kuo's field of study, I hold the highest opinion of his qualifications, and I am glad to offer this recommendation of his work."(Exhibit 3. Mr. XX, Database Administrator, XX University) (**Independent Advisory Opinion**)

Dr. Kuo has not only completed successful research in the field; his work has also gone on to influence his peers and colleagues. **Dr. Kuo's publications have been cited a total of XX times** according to Google Scholar, thereby demonstrating that these publications are widely recognized and relied upon in the field of information science.

Other noted experts confirm that Dr. Kuo's citation record indicates a demonstrated impact on the field that has well positioned him to continue to advance the endeavor:

> "Dr. Kuo has also been consistently well attuned to the needs of the research community, as evidenced by the nearly XX citations his work has amassed so far and the substantial amount of implementation his work has seen."(Exhibit 2. Dr. XX, Professor Emeritus, Dietrich College of Social Sciences, X University, Country)

> "Tellingly, Dr. Kuo's research has also been cited over a dozen times by individuals working in disciplines related to his work. Reaching such a number of citations while working in this highly specialized research area is a strong sign that Dr. Kuo ranks among the top talents working in his field today."(Exhibit 5. Mr. XX, Chief Executive Officer, XX Corporation) (**Independent Advisory Opinion**)

Dr. Kuo's specific contributions to the field further illustrate his expertise.

a. **A Computer-Aided Bibliometric System to Generate Core Article Ranked Lists in Interdisciplinary Subjects**

Dr. Kuo developed a novel computer aided bibliometric system in this project. Dr. Kuo's system is capable of constructing ordered lists within a core subject that cross various academic disciplines. Dr. Kuo's system allows for researchers to examine citations and papers with greater specificity, especially in multidisciplinary cases (Exhibits 1-6, publications). Dr. XX provides a more in-depth description of this project:

"At their core, bibliometrics systems are designed to impart useful information about research to their users, and computer-generated versions of these systems make use of technology to provide information in a more efficient and accessible manner than manual solutions. The information provided by Dr. Kuo's new system relates to important, pioneering, and milestone papers. Important papers are among the most highly cited in their category, while pioneering papers provide information about new subject matter, and milestone papers contain breakthrough discoveries that subsequently draw great attention from the field. Dr. Kuo used four proposed indicators, subject total cited counts (STCC), subject reference cited counts (SRCC) subject reference period impact, and subject reference cited history, to generate core article ranked lists in specific academic subjects. Dr. Kuo focused his subsequent research on the subjects of E-commerce, Data Mining, Supply Chain, Image Processing, Enterprise Resource Planning, Microarray, and Expert Systems. By analyzing the turning point patterns of each subject, Dr. Kuo found that three commonly held myths regarding published research were disproven by the data. The top ten papers in these subjects were not all submitted to Science Citation Index (SCI) journals, over 20% of papers with citation counts above 4 were also not submitted to SCI journals, and not all articles published in top journals were highly cited. This information is useful for individual researchers as well as for institutions, such as libraries, that purchase scientific journals and articles."(Exhibit 4. Dr. XX, Senior Lecturer in Business Analytics, XX Business School, University of XX) (**Independent Advisory Opinion**)

Dr. Kuo published 3 papers based on this project, which have received a total of **11 citations** (Exhibits publications, citations). One of these papers was published in *Information Sciences*, a journal with an **impact factor of 4.832** that is also **ranked #5** in Engineering and Computer Science (general) by Google Scholar (Exhibit [journal rankings]). Dr. Kuo's publication in this notable paper confirms that his work is highly important.

Dr. Kuo's research was cited by XX, who employed his work on data mining in order to conduct scientific literature classification (Exhibit [notable citations]). Dr. Kuo's work was also cited by XX et al., who based their i-index design on Dr. Kuo's findings (Exhibit notable citations). Finally, his work was also cited by XX, who employed his ranking and analysis methods in his studies (Exhibit notable citations). These citations provide strong evidence of the importance of Dr. Kuo's work, which has influenced the course of research in this area of study.

b. **Journal of Manuscript Submission Decision Support System**

Employing a variety of data theories and technology acceptance models, Dr. Kuo designed a system for the submission of academic papers to journals. He constructed his system according to the four principles of intelligence, design, choice, and implementation that make up a classic model for decision making, in addition to employing quantitative and qualitative analysis to confirm the high level of quality of his system (Exhibits 1-6, [publications]). Dr. XX and Dr. XX share their appraisals of this project:

- "I would like to comment further on the work Dr. Kuo has completed in the area of manuscript decision support systems. Because scholars must publish articles to maintain their positions in the field, getting prepared research accepted in academic venues is an essential task for those working in many research areas. However, not all journals use the same criteria for determining whether or not articles will be accepted, which makes navigating among the tens of thousands of venues that showcase new research a complex task. Dr. Kuo has constructed a support system for scholars searching for journals to publish their manuscripts. Using semantic retrieval, ontology, technology acceptance model, and other theories, Dr. Kuo analyzed information from the Web of Science database and

> *questionnaires sent to academic professionals. Equipped with this data, Dr. Kuo's system creates more individualized and accurate information about the journals likely to accept a user's work for publication."*(Exhibit 2. Dr. XX, Professor Emeritus, Dietrich College of Social Sciences, XX University, Country)

- *"One of Dr. Kuo's projects was aimed at direct support of researchers in academia. He gave several scholars, scientists, and other types of research professionals questionnaires to determine what factors affected acceptance of their articles in research publication. Dr. Kuo then collected the results and used this data, along with additional data from the Web of Science database, and looked for patterns in the data that were meaningful in determining the rationale for journals' accepting certain papers. Toward this end, Dr. Kuo employed ontological retrieval, text mining, and other methods, and he built his approach into a single manuscript submission decision support system. He found that 'similarity with types of papers accepted by the journal' and 'journal publishing group' were among the most salient factors in the fields of engineering and business management, but journal impact factor played a bigger role in engineering submissions than those in business management. Importantly, the completed system offers a way for scholars to streamline the journal selection process when submitting completed manuscripts, assisting their productivity and providing greater peace of mind. Kuo looked at research designated as cutting-edge by the National Science foundation, and found that obtaining similar results with algorithms was aided by filtering target terms. By focusing the tool on new terms, for instance, complexity and processing time are greatly reduced. The characteristics of this tool make it ideal for cutting time and labor costs for research and development tasks."*(Exhibit 6. Dr. XX, Engineering Director, XX Ltd.) (**Independent Advisory Opinion**)

Dr. Kuo published X papers, X international patents, and X U.S. patent application based on this project, which have received a total of **X citations** (Exhibits [publications, citations, U.S. patent, Taiwanese patents]). Dr. Kuo's work has been cited in three patents from companies including XX Ltd., XX Ltd., and XX Ltd. (Exhibit [notable citations]). In these citations, Dr. Kuo's system designs were employed as foundational design and methodology elements in the systems produced by these companies. His citations in this case display how critical his research is in the improvement of academic data systems.

c. **Research Analysis Methods and Systems**

In this project, Dr. Kuo implemented theories such as analytic hierarchy process theory, technology acceptance theory, and text mining in order to create a data analysis system for academic journals, papers, and news. Dr. Kuo's work included features such as creating indices for cutting edge reports and hot topics within various academic fields (Exhibits 1-6, publications). Dr. Tsai reports further on this research:

> *"Dr. Kuo has also combined text mining, analytic hierarchy process theory, and other approaches into a system for analyzing and forecasting the popularity of research topics. He has tested his system with many types of raw data, including academic papers and patents, and designed new indices for determining the popularity and current relevance of content based on terms contained within its text. This automates the process of determining what content qualifies as cutting edge, a traditionally time-consuming task, and the system is customizable. It allows its users to specify year and research fields and obtain detailed analytic reports describing the*

system's output."(Exhibit 2. Dr. X, Professor Emeritus, Dietrich College of Social Sciences, X University, Country)

Dr. Kuo published X papers, X Taiwanese patent, and X U.S. patent based on this project (Exhibits [publications, U.S. patent, Taiwanese patents]). One of these papers was published in *Information Sciences*, a journal with an **impact factor of 4.832** that is also **ranked #5** in engineering and computer science (general) by Google Scholar (Exhibit journal rankings). As with his other work, Dr. Kuo's acceptance in a highly regarded journal signifies the critical necessity of his contributions.

As further confirmation of the importance of this project, it was funded by the Ministry of Science and Technology (MOST) of the Republic of China (Exhibit proof of MOST funding). The interest of a major national agency in Dr. Kuo's work proves that his research is of great importance.

d. **Taiwan Science Citation Index System**

Dr. Kuo developed and created an indexing service for citations of Taiwanese journals. In this project, he employed novel bibliometrics, including distributed system and artificial intelligence networks in order to provide a user friendly and intuitive system. He also ensured that the system was able to generate keywords from field dictions, among other useful functionalities (Exhibits 1-6, [publications]). Dr. Chang expounds:

> *"One such achievement is Dr. Kuo's novel system for evaluating the research performance of journals in Taiwan, called the Taiwan Science Citation Index System. This system leverages bibliometrics, statistics, AI, and text mining techniques to analyze journal performance. To make the system operational, Dr. Kuo created novel metadata formats from source articles and designed new research indices. These include the journal international impact index, journal cheat index, journal subscription recommendation index, and scholar confidence index. Some other capabilities that Dr. Kuo included in his system are generation of classic and original paper designations, classification of the most popular and trending subjects, generation of keywords from field dictionaries, and identification of researchers as award candidates based on objective data. Dr. Kuo was given a research budget from the National Science Foundation and ScholarWorld Corporation to apply his system to the corpus of research in certain scientific fields in Taiwan. The information he has provided supplements existing databases covering social science and art citations in the country. After collecting around 400,000 references and building his database, Dr. Kuo generated Journal Citation Report information for 220 Taiwanese scientific journals. He found that the average impact factor of these journals is 0.18. His work provides a function similar to that provided by Web of Science for English language journals and articles. Many professionals representing journals in Taiwan have already contacted Dr. Kuo to get their journals added to the indexing system he created."*(Exhibit 1. Dr. XX, Professor, Department of XX Engineering, XX University)

Dr. Kuo published X papers based on this project (Exhibits [publications]). Additionally, the XX based their hospital assessment laws on the evaluation of medical doctors' publications on Dr. Kuo's system (Exhibit [proof of XX implementation]). The implementation of Dr. Kuo's work in Taiwan's laws shows the outstanding quality of his work.

e. **Critical Technological Applications of Smartphones**

In this project, Dr. Kuo designed new intelligent applications for smartphones. His applications exist in a variety of areas, including in utility areas such as speakers, mobile network management systems, mobile travel assistance, and so on. The work employs a number of theories, including TRIZ, mind map, and intelligent system, to improve the usability of these devices (Exhibits 1-6, [publications]). Mr. XX speaks further on this topic:

> "In one of his projects, Dr. Kuo constructed systems integrating Smartphone software and hardware oriented toward specific tasks and interfaces. These include a system for conducting Smartphone-assisted group tours, a loudspeaker System for mobile digital broadcasts, Smartphone integration with geographic information systems for virtual sports, a Smartphone digital fax system, and more. This project has led to 17 distinct patent ideas that have been purchased and are being patented and commercialized. One idea that has already led to a written patent application is the Smartphone-assisted group tour system. This System includes several subsystem and modules. There are modules for facilitating tourist procurement, models for managing tips given to tour guides, a module for completing customer satisfaction surveys, etc. There are also modules written for stores to recommend specific products to tour groups with customized recommendations and analytics tools for improving the overall experience."(Exhibit 3. Mr. XX, Database Administrator, XX University) (**Independent Advisory Opinion**)

Two of Dr. Kuo's XX pending Chinese patents that he developed as a part of this project have been purchased by XX Corporation (a subsidiary of XX Technology Inc.) (Exhibit [Chinese patent, proof of XX Corporation patent purchase]). The purchase and commercialization of Dr. Kuo's smartphone applications proves that his work is valuable and sought after, as well as highly novel.

f. **Pen Reader with Wireless Transmission Function**

Dr. Kuo designed a wireless pen reader which scans documents and transmits them to a device such as a tablet or computer. Dr. Kuo's design has numerous applications in multi-media e-learning as well as in business. The pen utilizes Bluetooth and wifi connections to transfer its data, providing a simple and cost-effective solution to storage transfer (Exhibits 1-6, [publications]). Mr. XX comments in Dr. Kuo's design and development of this item:

> "The patent of his that was purchased by my company contains technology for a talking pen to interact with Smartphone and tablet devices. Talking pens operate by giving character or letter pronunciations and other educational information related to the text with which the pen interacts. However, talking pens typically include only a speaker for interacting with users, which is to say that other types of media like photos and videos are not usually accessible with this technology, Dr. Kuo designed a new variety of talking pen that includes Bluetooth or wifi connections to connect with smartphones and tablets. This uses the devices data connection to pull content from the cloud when triggered by a signal from the smart pen. This sort of data connection means that very little data actually needs to be stored on the pen itself, which saves money on storage card and battery costs. The pen also has the capability of using the connected device for its audio needs, eliminating the need for a speaker in the pen itself. In this way, Dr. Kuo's design lowers cost and weight requirements while expanding capabilities, an impressive accomplishment."(Exhibit 5. Mr. XX, Chief Executive Officer, XX Corporation) (**Independent Advisory Opinion**)

Dr. Kuo has published X patent based on this project (Exhibit [Taiwanese patents]). Recently, Dr. Kuo's patent was purchased by XX Corporation in order to produce and sell Dr. Kuo's pen (Exhibit [proof of XX Corporation patent purchase]). The sale of Dr. Kuo's device once again highlights how excellent Dr. Kuo's research and design work is.

Dr. Kuo is also active in the scientific community as a peer reviewer for highly acclaimed journals (Exhibit [peer review]). Dr. Kuo has already conducted at least X reviews, including reviews for *Information Sciences*, *Program*, *Computers and Electrical Engineering*, *Engineering Computations*, and *Scientometrics*. Only top-level experts in their field are invited to perform this important review work, so this frequent review activity further demonstrates Dr. Kuo's important standing in the field.

In recognition of the value and importance of his work, Dr. Kuo has also been granted funding from leading agencies (Exhibit [funding]). These grants include numerous instances of funding from the Ministry of Science and Technology (MOST) of the Republic of China (Exhibit proof of MOST funding).The financial support of Dr. Kuo's work by this organization demonstrates the importance of his research.

Thus, the significance of Dr. Kuo's work in his field is corroborated by evidence of peer interest in his research. Dr. Kuo's education, experience, and expertise in his field, the significance of his contributions, and his past record of success position him well to continue to advance his proposed endeavor of computer-aided bibliometric systems.Dr. Kuo therefore satisfies this prong.

IV. On balance, it would be beneficial to the United States to waive the requirements of a job offer and thus of a labor certification

As discussed above, Dr. Kuo holds 2 advanced degrees in a field tied to the proposed endeavor, and the submitted evidence demonstrates that he possesses considerable experience and expertise in a highly specialized field (Exhibit [CV, degrees]). The evidence also shows that research on computer-aided bibliometric systems holds significant implications for the advancement of database and research technology. Because of his record of successful research in an area that furthers U.S. interests, Dr. Kuo offers contributions of such value that, on balance, they would benefit the United States even assuming other qualified U.S. workers are available. Dr. Kuo therefore satisfies this prong.

V. Conclusion

As the documentary evidence and corroborating testimony from experts in the field establishes, Dr. Kuo is a member of the professions holding an advanced degree. He proposes to continue his research on computer-aided bibliometric systems, which is clearly an endeavor with substantial merit and national importance. His education, experience, and expertise, record of publication and citation, and history of successful research in the field all indicate that Dr. Kuo is well positioned to benefit the proposed endeavor. These facts establish that it is beneficial to the United States to waive the requirements of a job offer and labor certification. Dr. Kuo has therefore established eligibility for and otherwise merits a national interest waiver, and his petition should be approved.

INDEX OF EXHIBITS

<u>Letters of Recommendation</u>

Exhibit 1	Letter & CV from Dr. XX, Professor, Department of XX Engineering, XX University
Exhibit 2	Letter & CV from Dr. XX, Professor Emeritus, Dietrich College of Social Sciences, XX University, Country
Exhibit 3	Letter & CV from Mr. X, Database Administrator, XX University (**Independent Advisory Opinion**)
Exhibit 4	Letter & CV from Dr. XX, Senior Lecturer in Business Analytics, XX Business School, University of XX (**Independent Advisory Opinion**)
Exhibit 5	Letter & CV from Mr. XX, Chief Executive Officer, XX Corporation (**Independent Advisory Opinion**)
Exhibit 6	Letter & CV from Dr. XX, Engineering Director, XX Ltd. (**Independent Advisory Opinion**)

<u>Academic and Professional Background</u>

Exhibit 7	Dr. Kuo's CV
Exhibit 8	Copy of Dr. Kuo's Ph.D. diploma, academic transcripts, and degree evaluation
Exhibit 9	Copies of Dr. Kuo's additional diplomas (M.Sc., B.Sc.)
Exhibit 10	Personal statement describing Dr. Kuo's proposed research endeavors in the United States

Peer-reviewed Publications and Citations

Exhibit 11   Peer-reviewed article authored by Dr. Kuo, "A computer-aided bibliometrics system for journal citation analysis and departmental core journal ranking list generation," *Journal of Educational Media & Library Sources*, 2004 & testimonial confirming Dr. Kuo's participation on the project

Exhibit 12   Peer-reviewed article authored by Dr. Kuo, "Textbook Assessment Method and System – The Example of Information Management Textbooks," *Journal of Southern Taiwan University of Science and Technology: Social Science Edition*, 2017

Exhibit 13   Peer-reviewed article authored by Dr. Kuo, "The Ingredients Recommended Method and System for Meal Research and Development," *Information and Management Science*, 2016

Exhibit 14   Peer-reviewed article authored by Dr. Kuo, "Use of the Taiwan Patent Search System to Analyze Stock Market," *NCKU Library Journal*, 2016

Exhibit 15   Peer-reviewed article authored by Dr. Kuo, "The Recommendation Method for Oral Exam Committee," *Information and Management Science*, 2015

Exhibit 16   Peer-reviewed article authored by Dr. Kuo, "An Application of the UTAUT Model to Explore the Using Cloud Web Storage Behavior: A Case Study of Dropbox," *Information and Management Science*, 2014

Exhibit 17   Peer-reviewed article authored by Dr. Kuo, "The Hot and Looking Forward Research Analysis in the Information Management Field Between 2006 to 2010," *Information and Management Science*, 2012

Exhibit 18   Peer-reviewed article authored by Dr. Kuo, "The Effects of Web Usability on Trust and Continuance Intention of Group Buying Site Users," *Information and Management Science*, 2012

Exhibit 19   Peer-reviewed article authored by Dr. Kuo, "Software Development and EvaluationSoftware Development and Evaluation Model-A Case Study of Apple App Store," *Information and Management Science*, 2011

Exhibit 20   Peer-reviewed article authored by Dr. Kuo, "The Patent Analysis and System for Taiwan University and Colleage Between 2007 and 2009," *Information and Management Science*, 2009

Exhibit 21   Evidence of Dr. Kuo's other articles (54)

Exhibit 22   Book authored by Dr. Kuo, *The Analysis and Introduction of English Core Journal and Thesis Between 1998 to 2008*, ScholarWorld Press, 2012

Exhibit 23   Book authored by Dr. Kuo, *The Business Management Lesson Learnt from Biology*, ScholarWorld Press, 2012

Exhibit 24   Evidence of Dr. Kuo's U.S. patent

Exhibit 25   Evidence of Dr. Kuo's U.S. patent application

Exhibit 26	Evidence of Dr. Kuo's Chinese patent
Exhibit 27	Evidence of Dr. Kuo's 10 Taiwanese patents
Exhibit 28	Evidence of Dr. Kuos other Taiwanese patents (353)
Exhibit 29	Relevant rankings of publications that have featured Dr. Kuo's work
Exhibit 30	Dr. Kuo's overall Google Scholar citation record
Exhibit 31	Notable citations of Dr. Kuo's work (Yen; XX et al.; XX; XX Ltd.; Hitachi Ltd.; XX Ltd.)

Other

Exhibit 32	Evidence of Dr. Kuo's peer review service
Exhibit 33	Evidence of Dr. Kuo's funding from the Ministry of Science and Technology (MOST) of the Republic of China
Exhibit 34	Evidence of the implementation of Dr. Kuo's work by the XX
Exhibit 35	Evidence of the purchase of Dr. Kuo's patent by XX Corporation
Exhibit 36	Evidence of the purchase of Dr. Kuo's patent by XX Corporation
Exhibit 37	Jisc page on the importance of search engines in academic research
Exhibit 38	Pew Research Center page on the use of the internet in the United States

2) Personal Statement Example

Date: XX/XX/2018

To: USCIS

Background

My career in computer science began in 1999 with the beginning of my research work at the Chunghwa Telecom Laboratories. During this time, I developed an extensive skill, focusing mostly on the development and usage of various software theories and applications, as well as extensive study of data mining for scientific literature. This was the major focus of my doctoral research at National Central University's department of Information Management. IDC (International Data Corporation) says that worldwide revenues for big data(data mining) and business analytics will grow from $130.1 billion in 2016 to more than $203 billion in 2020, at a compound annual growth rate (CAGR) of 11.7%. In addition to being the industry with the largest investment in big data and business analytics solutions (nearly $17 billion in 2016), banking will see the fastest spending growth. As such, this is a research area of substantial international interest.

My research has particularly focused on text mining for scientific literatures. One of my first major research projects involved the development of new models for determining the department and subject core journal ranking list by computer-aided bibliometrics system. Through this work, I was able to identify the optimal journal ranking for departments and fields by computer automatically. This work was subsequently impact to Web of Science. Currently, Web of Science also begins to provide the category and field journal ranking for scholars.

After completing my doctoral degree at NCU, I turned my focus to journal manuscript submission decision support system. This research patent was cited by many big companies in google patent database including Elsevier, Hitachi, China Unionpay Ltd. and so on. IEEE has just use my idea to provide a website service. Its name is *IEEE Publication Recommender*. The journal publisher giant, Elsevier Ltd. also use this to provide one product to the global. The product name is *Journal Finder*. These services are directly based upon my research.

Though I was working outside the United States, I received many invitations letters to review articles for leading international journals in my research field such as Scientometrics, Information Sciences, Program and so on. I also received several invited key session speaker for international conferences such as 2017 ISACIT Computing and Information Conference, 4th International Conference On Multidisciplinary Trends In Academic Research and so on.

Thus far, I have published 20 peer-reviewed articles in the leading journals in my field, including one article in *Information Sciences (SCI) and another in Program (SSCI)*. I have also published 44 articles in major conference proceedings, including International Conference on Machine Learning and Computing, IEEE, China, and have authored a book for *The Analysis and Introduction of English Core Journal and Thesis Between 1998 to 2008 (ISBN:* 978-986-87200-1-5). I have also owned over 350 patens in Taiwan, China and USA. My innovation work has also been directly implemented by many industry companies such as a leading international publisher Elsevier Ltd's Journal Finder or the Lion Bubboe tour app provided by largest traveling agency (Lion travel) in Taiwan. I also sold many my patents to international company such as XX Ltd. and XX Ltd. Therefore I am confident that it will continue to have a considerable impact upon the field in the United States and beyond.

Future Research Plans

In the coming years, I intend to extend my research on computer-aided bibliometrics methodology, text mining and legal information system. Particular challenges in the field of bibliometrics was to design new useful evaluation index, visualization tools, journal information retrieval, open access journal solution and so on. In my future work, I intend to extend my prior experiments and innovation to cover additional scientific literature bibliometrics system and computer added-value legal system.

1. Apply Artificial Intelligence Technology to Journal Manuscript Submission Decision Support System

One area I would like to extend my research on is the integration of artificial intelligence methodology with journal article submission decision support system. Owing to the past experiences, many people are interested in my journal manuscript submission decision support system including Elsevier Ltd, IEEE, Edanz Group Ltd and so on. Therefore, I plan to do more researches on this subject. The ontology in artificial intelligence (AI) would be a good direction to enhance the system. Currently, I am cooperating with NCKU professor to apply ontology methodology on patent information retrieval system now. In the future, I intend to transfer my previous relation database to owl and ontology. Redefine the schema with RDF and use JENA API to integrate with my previous ASP.net. codes. RDF Query Language SPARQL would be used to replace SQL to proceed with intelligent query. This would make system more useful and easy to use. Advance publication, patent and product could be extended.

2: The add-valued system to search results from academic journal search engine and information retrieval

Most search engines or information retrieval systems are focus on generating search results from end user's the input terms or inquiry condition. I plan to develop more advanced add-valued analysis or usage from general search results. There are several potential applications including 1)Looking forward research intelligence and latest hot research subjects analysis method and system, 2)Professional field dictionary with computer aided vocabulary collection and generation, 3)Original, milestone and pioneer articles filter and recommend system, 4)Outstanding and pioneer scholars filter and recommend system. There are still many other innovation methods and systems can be explored and integrated with traditional search engine to provide more rich and variable information for end users.

3: The legal information management and application method and system

Compared with other fields, there are very few information science scholars or computer scientist who do the research or develop new system in the field of legal. The journal publication, patent and software related to the legal information system are seldom in the past. I have several publications and patents in the legal subject area were published before. They are as the following: 1)The law office and lawyer recommendation method and system (one master thesis, one conference paper and one patent), 2)The drug sentencing decision support system(one patent, one conference paper), 3)The intellectual property sentence calculator (one master thesis, one conference paper and one patent), 4)Legal document computer-aided generation method and system.(one patent). There are still many interesting subjects I want to proceed with research and development such as: parole threshold decision support system, assigned to prison decision support system, the state compensation of miscarriage of justice calculator, the immigration case information management system and so on.

Future Job Opportunities

In order to accomplish my research goals, I have been seeking opportunities to go to the United States and continue my work there. I am currently in contact with Dr. XX, professor at the XX University. Having heard of my work, he has suggested that I can try to apply for a position at the XX University. (the scanned letter attached).

The Technical Recruiter in XX, Inc., XX, he saw my profile and inquiry me whether I am interested in working at their company or not. XX provide IT solutions for the financial, energy, healthcare and insurance industries. XX can provide employees at least 401K. XX has 10 locations in USA. And XX has another locations in Switzerland and U.K. (scanned Email attached).

The XX in Diverse XX, XX sent one email to me for one permanent position. The job title is Data Scientist. The location is at Brandenton, FL. The skills for this job are advanced programming skills in R and expertise in machine learning. XX Inc. was established in 2002. They were head quartered in XX with an off-shore delivery center in New Delhi, India. The Delivery Center is 250+ associate strong and operates on a 24/7 model. They have covered from Big Data to infrastructure upgrades, social media to mainframes and process improvement to app replacement. (the scanned Email attached).

Based upon my prior success in the field of computer science and my overall reputation, I am certain of my ability to find suitable employment within my field in the United States once I receive my visa. Considering the impact my work has had thus far, I am confident that my work will continue to positively influence the field and the United States in the future.

Sincerely,

_____

3) The Example of Equal Contribution with the First Author

[Please insert date of signature]

Dear Adjudicating Officer,

I am writing to offer you evidence of Dr. Min Chien Kuo's substantial contributions to the article "A computer-aided bibliometrics system for journal citation analysis and departmental core journal ranking list generation," published in a 2014 edition of the *Journal of XXX*. I am pleased to testify that Dr. Kuo was a significant contributor and co-author of this work.

This study has been cited a total of XX times, testifying to its worth in the scientific community. The article describes our creation of a computer-aided bibliometrics system that generates ranked core journal lists for specific academic departments based on journal performance. This assessment of performance includes automated evaluations of journal citations and queries from online readers belonging to the same academic department, and our system performs favorably compared to competing methods. The data provided by this system is useful for libraries that must determine which journals subscriptions ought to be retained and which ought to be dropped to ensure the most effective use of funds.

This work is important to the field of information science because serial academic publications have proliferated by unprecedented amounts in recent years. This process has made it increasingly difficult for departments and libraries to prioritize publications for subscription, especially when limited budgets and increasing subscription costs are taken into consideration. Our work uses algorithms and bibliometrics methodologies to create ranked lists of journals for individual departments, giving users of our system a means to make the most effective use of their subscription funds. By extension, our work benefits the education sector as a whole, since students also benefit from the enhanced efficiency our system provides.

Dr. Kuo and I collaborated extensively on this project. I may be listed as the primary author of this work, but I am more than willing to uphold that Dr. Kuo was an essential member of the team. As a co-author of the article, he made contributions equal to my own. Conventional wisdom might hold that the first listed author of the article should receive the majority of the credit for the work, but that was not the case for this project. Dr. Kuo was just as influential as I was in terms of the overall effort made and the final outcome. In our work together, I personally observed Dr. Kuo's significant skills in the field of information science. His leadership, innovative spirit, and expert understanding of the subject matter were all key factors in this project's success.

I would be happy to answer any further questions you may have about this case. Should any arise, please contact me directly.

Most Sincerely,

XXX

CHAPTER VI. EXHIBIT FOR SUPPORTING DOCUMENTS

You should prepare supporting documents for your petition letter. Many of these documents need to be collected and then mailed to the lawyer if you hire one. I have listed some examples below:

1) Professional Background

Applicants need to prepare their diplomas, as shown in Figure 6-1. You can include all the diplomas you have earned, including bachelor's, master's, and Ph.D.

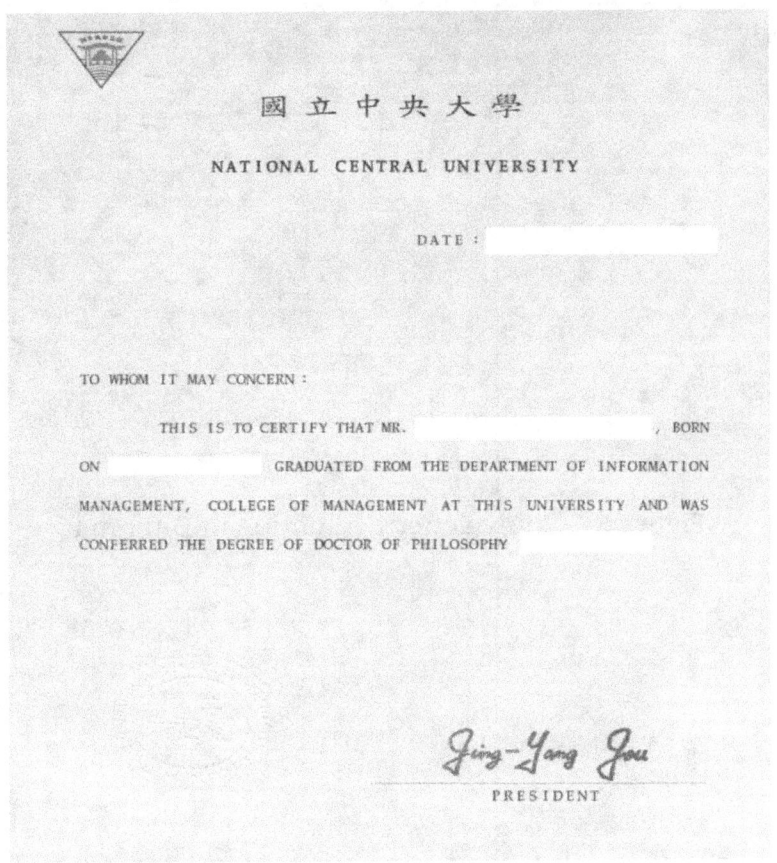

Figure 6-1 Diploma

2) Equivalency Evaluation of Diploma

Applicants need to apply for an equivalency evaluation of their diploma if they did not receive it in the United States. Some organizations provide this service, such as World Education Services. Figure 6-2 is a sample. This evaluation will cost about 100 dollars.

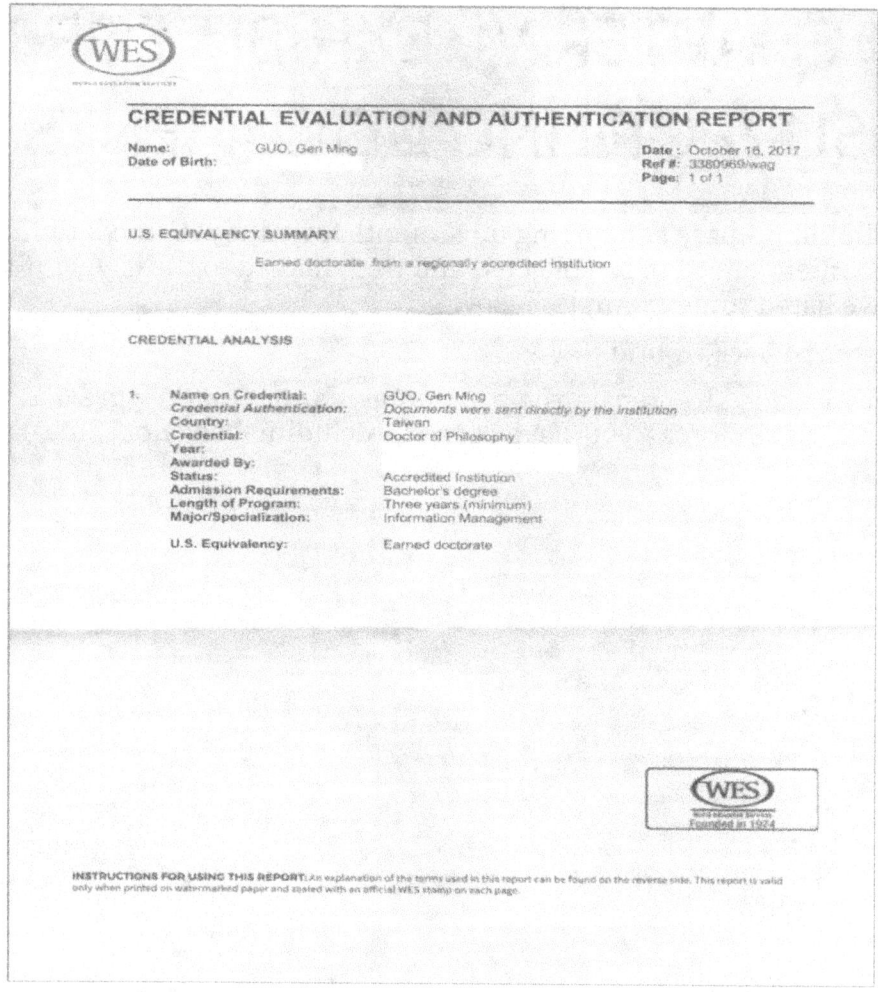

Figure 6-2 Equivalency Evaluation of Diploma

3) Affidavit for different appearance of names

If you have had different names in the past, you need to write a letter and sign your name as shown in Figure 6-3. I have had many names because several of my patent agents spelled my English name from my Chinese name in different ways. When I prepared the supporting documents, I found more and more variations of my name. I updated this form from two names to seven names in the past.

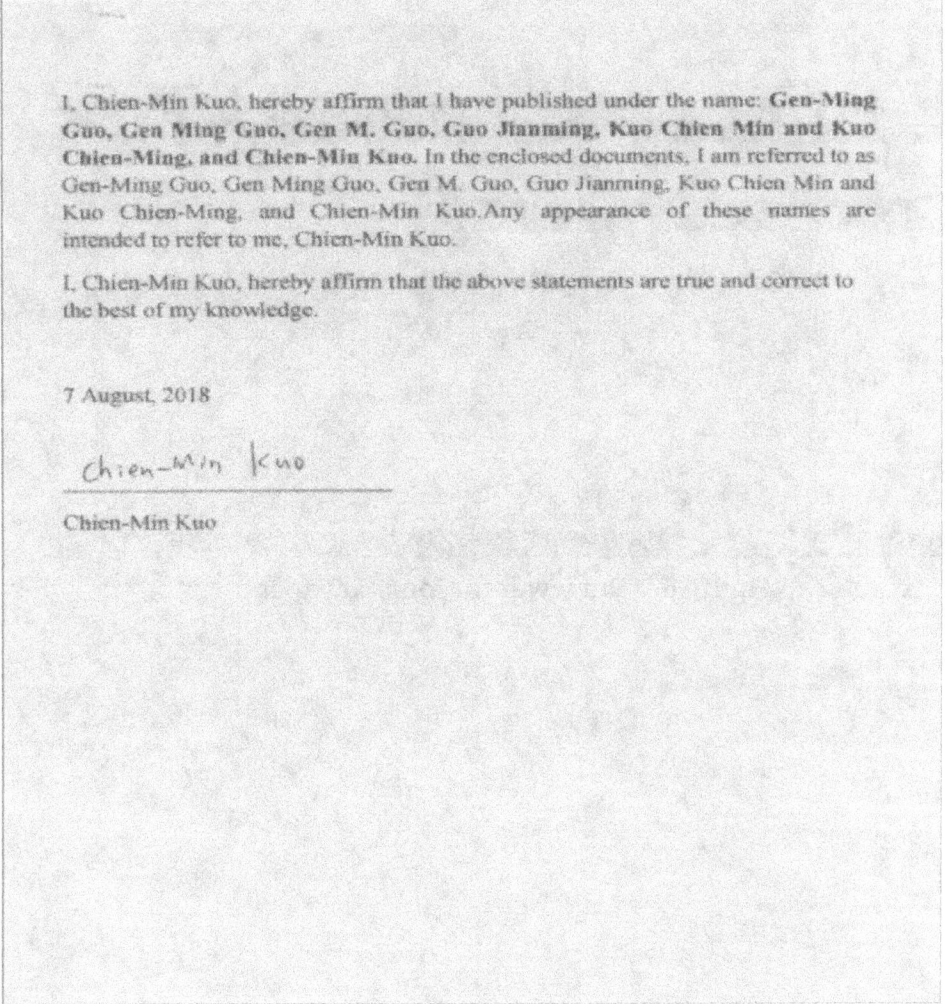

Figure 6-3 Affidavit for Different Names

4) Paper Reviewer

It is not enough to prepare the evidence showing you accepted the invitation to review an academic journal paper. You should also prepare evidence that you completed the reviewer assignments, as shown in Figure 6-4. Some people accept the invitation but do not finish the work. Sometimes, the editor will cancel the assignment during the review process. Therefore, you need to prepare the complete reviewer assignments.

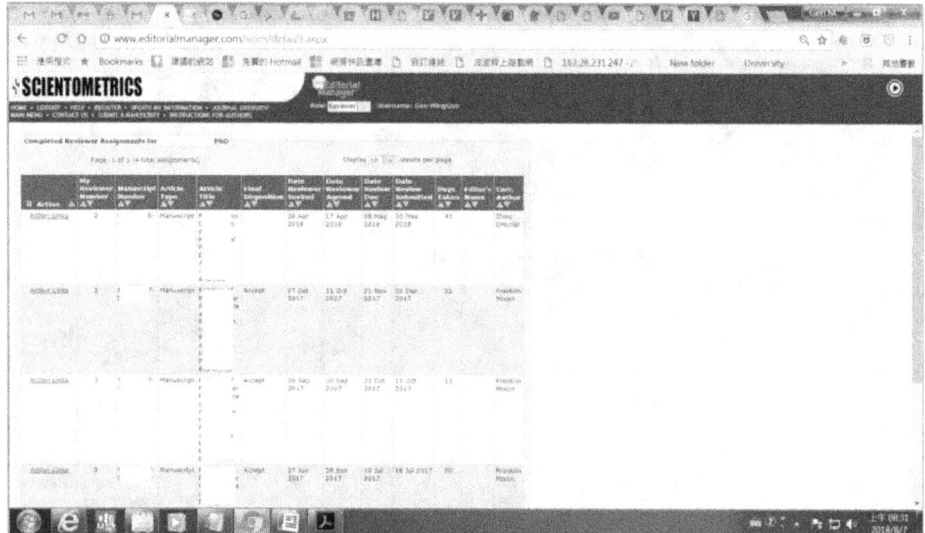

Figure 6-4 Reviewer for Journal Paper

5) Job Offer or Opportunity

If you receive a job offer, it is very beneficial. You can print it as your supporting document. If you do not have a job offer, you can use a job opportunity letter instead. Please see the example in Figure 6-5.

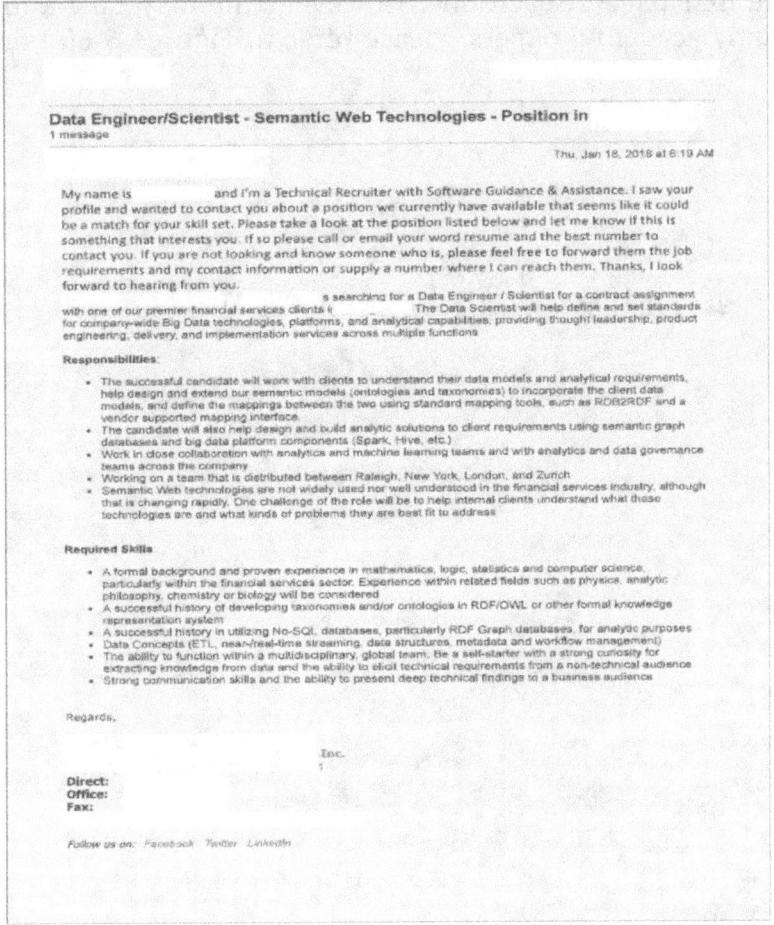

Figure 6-5 Job Opportunity Letter

6) Academic Paper

You can print your published conference papers and journal papers as supporting documents. You only need to print the front pages for each paper. Your name and related information, such as date, source, volume, issue, and page, must be included. If your articles were not published in English, you can translate the first page of each one. However, this may take a lot of time if you have many academic papers. Please refer to Figures 6-6(a) and 6-6(b) as examples.

郭建明等／南臺學報社會科學類 第2卷第1期 2017年6月88–114 88

教科書評鑑方法與系統—以資訊管理教科書為例

*郭建明[1]、林意晴[2]

[1]南臺科技大學資訊管理系

[2]國立成功大學圖書館

*sambuela@stust.edu.tw

摘要

教科書排序評鑑方法與系統，其主要係以運用博碩士論文與期刊論文的參考文獻之引用教科書狀況，以及教科書間的交叉引用，所設計出來的論文引用指數與引用排名報告來令使用者得知該教科書被引用度與評價高低；同時輔助採用圖書館借閱流通記錄、問卷調查與評比及教師採用教科書的整合型綜合指數，用以更清楚得知該教科書的評價狀況與被引用指數，同時亦能夠提供兩者之間的比較分析與效果驗證，使得排序評鑑方法與資訊系統的設計能更加完善精確，藉以有效提供教師、學生與圖書館員在篩選與選購教科書時的一種電腦輔助計量決策與推薦工具。

關鍵詞：教科書、評鑑、文獻計量

Figure 6-6(a) Chinese Journal Paper

Textbook Assessment Method and System – The Example of Information Management Textbooks

*Gen Ming, Guo[1], Yi Ching, Lin[2]

[1*]Department of Information Management, Southern Taiwan University of Science and Technology
[2]Library, National Cheng Kung University

Abstract

For this study, we designed an assessment method and system for textbook ranking. The proposed approach mainly references master's and doctor's theses and the periodical papers which cite textbooks as well as references cited among textbooks themselves. The designed citing index and citing report may help scholars to better assess textbook quality and how often it is cited. The textbook circulation records in the library and a questionnaire for professors are also used in the composite index of the textbook assessment. This would help scholars more understand the quality of different textbooks. These methods offer more comparative analysis, and verify the results between them, and also allow the design of more accurate methods for evaluating and ranking information systems. The proposed method and system can also provide introduction tools and computerized auxiliary measures for teachers, students, and library staff when screening and buying textbooks.

Keywords: Textbook, Assessment, Bibliometrics

Received: Aug. 10, 2016; first revised: Jan. 19, 2017; accepted: Jun. 2017.
Corresponding author: G. M. Guo, Department of Information Management, Southern Taiwan University of Science and Technology, Tainan, Taiwan.

Figure 6-6(b) English Translation

7) Birth Certification

If you have the birth certificate in English as shown in Figure 6-7(a), it is very convenient. However, if you only have the birth certificate in another language as shown in Figure 6-7(b), you will need to translate it into English, as shown in Figure 6-7(c). After completing the translation, you should find a suitable place to notarize it, as shown in Figure 6-7(d). Notarizing your birth certificate will incur some costs. Some travel agents can help customers by taking the document to the Ministry of Foreign Affairs for a fee. Therefore, you can try seeking help from them.

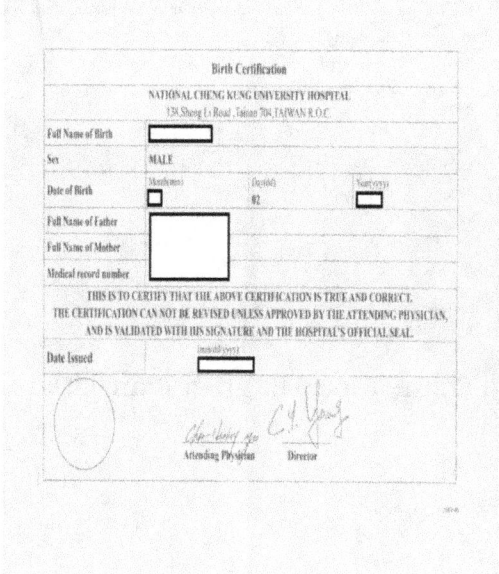

Figure 6-7(a) Birth Certificate

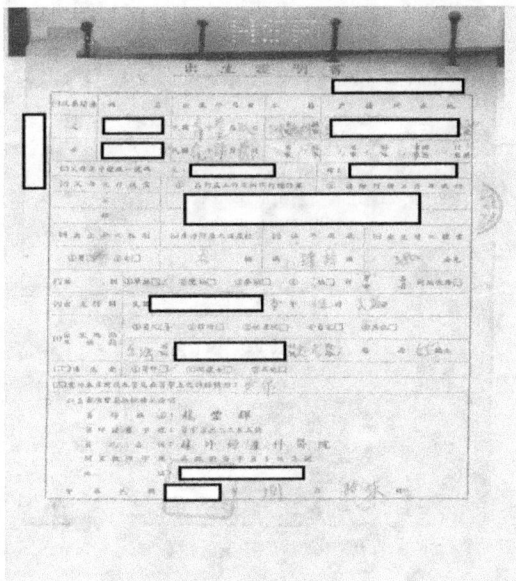

Figure 6-7(b) Original Birth Certificate

Figure 6-7(c) Translated Certificate

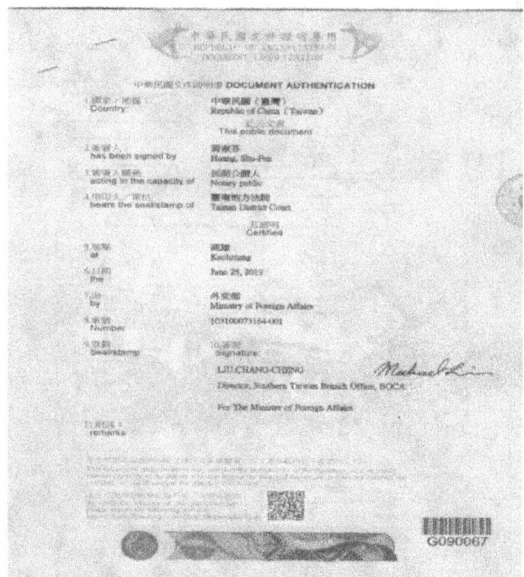

Figure 6-7(d) Notarized Certificate

8) Patent

You can prepare the published patent documents as shown in Figures 6-8(a) and 6-8(b). For domestic patents, you should find the English version on your local patent and trademark office's patent search website. If you cannot find the English version, you will have to translate the original document into English.

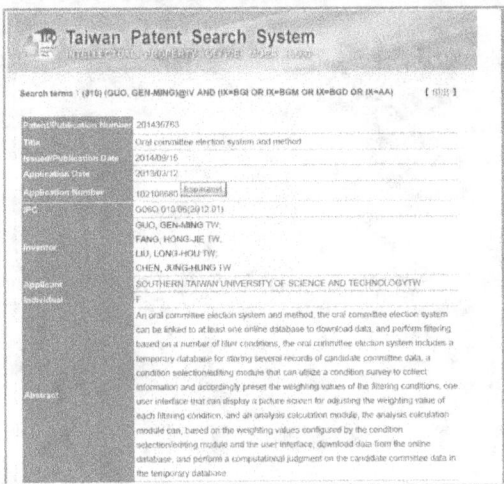

Figure 6-8(a) Domestic Patent

Figure 6-8(b) U.S.A. Patent

9) Award

USCIS prefers international awards over domestic ones. Therefore, you should try to participate in international competitions and obtain international awards. I have many domestic awards, but my lawyer did not use any of them.

10) Project

You can prepare evidence for all kinds of projects you have undertaken before. For example, government projects, company-assigned projects, patent procurement, and so on. Figures 6-9(a) and 6-9(b) show the patent transfer project contract, and Figure 6-9(c) is its translated version. All documents must provide an English version along with the original version.

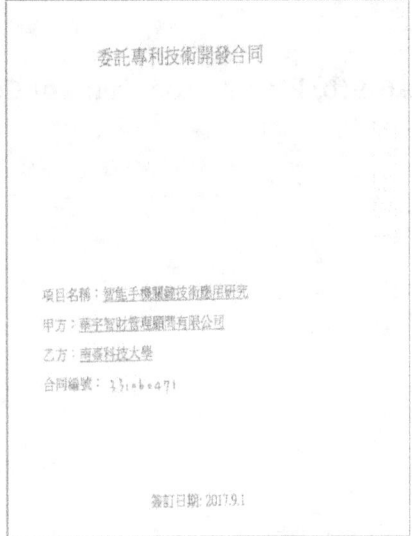

Figure 6-9(a) Contract Cover

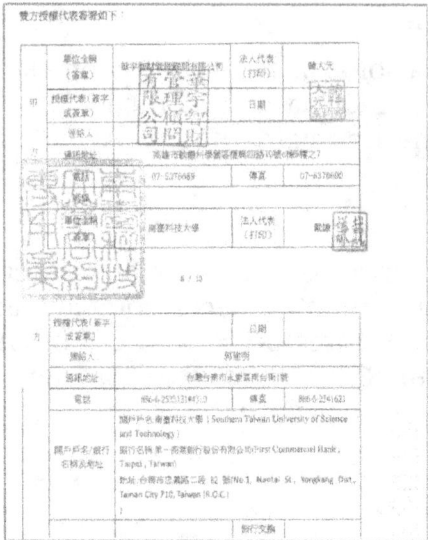

Figure 6-9(b) Patent Procurement Contract

colspan Entrust Patent Technique Development Contract

Contract Name: <u>Smartphone Critical Technique R&D</u>
Party A: <u>HUA-YU Intellectual Property Management Consulting Company Limited</u>
Party B: <u>Southern Taiwan University of Science and Technology</u>
Contract No: 331060471

Contract Date: Sep. 1, 2017
Authorized representatives of both parties:

Party A	Organization	HUA-YU Intellectual Property Management Consulting Company Limited	Legal Representatives	Han, Da-Yuan
	Authorized Representatives	Han, Da-Yuan	Date	
	Contact	Han, Da-Yuan		
	Address	No.10, Fuxing 4th Rd., Qianzhen Dist., Kaohsiung City, Taiwan		
	Phone	07-5376689	Fax	07-5376690
	Postal Code	806		
Party B	Organization	Southern Taiwan University of Science and Technology	Legal Representatives	Dai Cian
	Authorized Representatives	Kuo Chien-Min	Date	
	Contact	Kuo Chien-Min		
	Address	No. 1. Nantai St., Yongkang Dist., Tainan City 710, Taiwan		
	Phone	0755-86095550-8550	Fax	0755-86095550-8801
	Account/Bank Name/Address	Account Name: Southern Taiwan University of Science and Technology Bank Name: First Commercial Bank, Taipei, Taiwan Address: No. 1. Nantai St., Yongkang Dist., Tainan City 710, Taiwan		
	Account	601-50-08833-1	SWIFT Code	FCBKTWTPXXX

Figure 6-9(c) Patent Procurement Contract Translation

11) Job Invitation

It is better to prepare a job offer or job invitation document (Figure 6-10), although it is not necessary for the NIW category. Applicants can apply from abroad without an employer, which is an advantage of this category. However, when you pass the I-140 review process, the consulate officer will ask for this during your interview. Therefore, you should try to obtain a job offer or job invitation at an early stage.

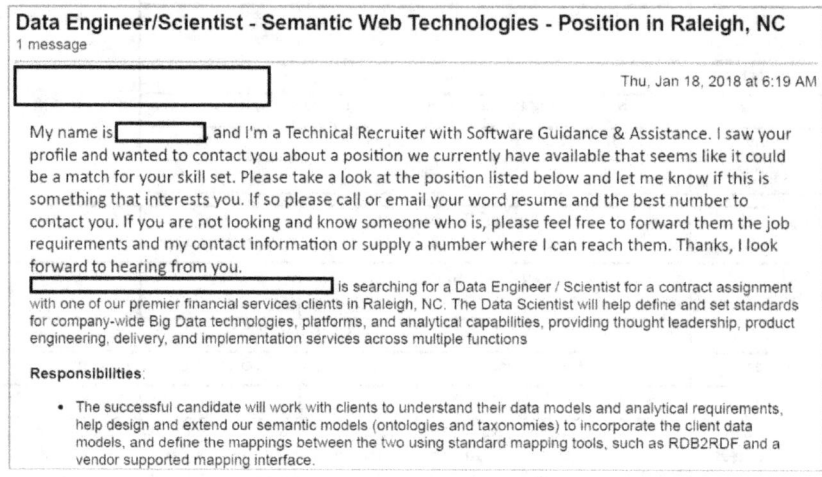

Figure 6-10 Job Invitation

CHAPTER VII. FILE THE CASE

After you pay the fee and file the case, you will receive Form I-797C as shown in Figure 7-1. This receipt contains three important pieces of information: 1) Receipt number, 2) Received date, and 3) Priority date. Generally, you will need to inquire about your case status regularly. You will need this information to do so. Most people have to wait more than six months. Given this long wait, applicants often want to inquire about their case status. You can input your receipt number at the following website (Figure 7-2): https://egov.uscis.gov/casestatus/landing.do. As for the *received date* and *priority date*, it is used to inquiry the visa bulletin. Please refer to chapter 10 for the detail.

If there are any issues with your I-140 petition, you will receive a notice from USCIS for an RFE (Request for Evidence). In this situation, USCIS will request additional evidence to support parts of your I-140 petition. The petition will be rejected by USCIS if you do not respond within the indicated days.

Figure 7-1 The Receipt For Filing The Case.

GET E2/EB2/NIW GREEN CARD FROM ABROAD WITH LOW BUDGET

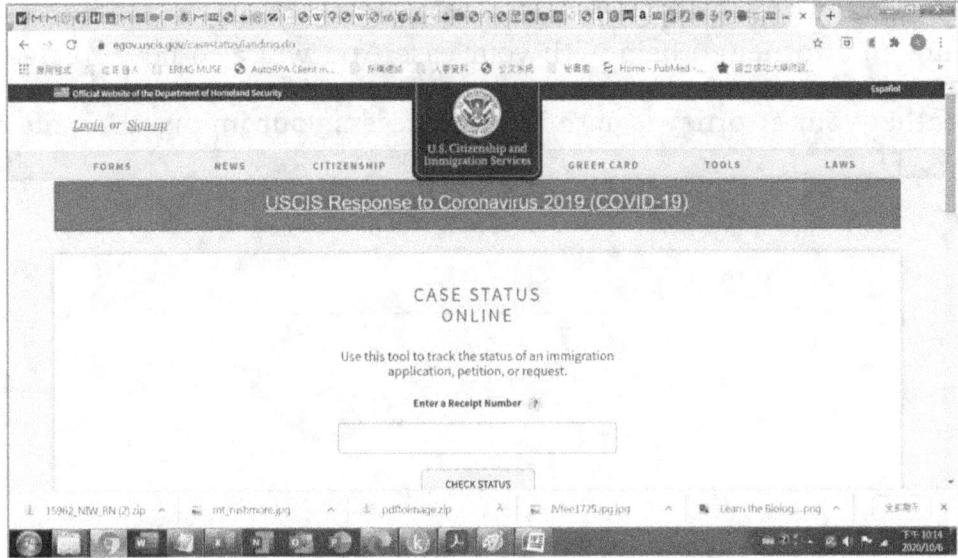

Figure 7-2 Check Status For Your Case Online.

When should you sign and submit Form G-28? You will sign this form if you hire an attorney to help with your case. You will also need to sign and submit this form if you change to a new attorney. After you sign this form, it means that your attorney is authorized to access your immigration file from USCIS.

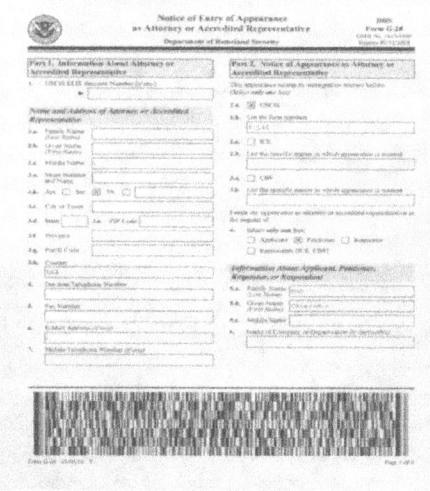

Figure 7-3(a) Form G-28 (1/3)

GET E2/EB2/NIW GREEN CARD FROM ABROAD WITH LOW BUDGET

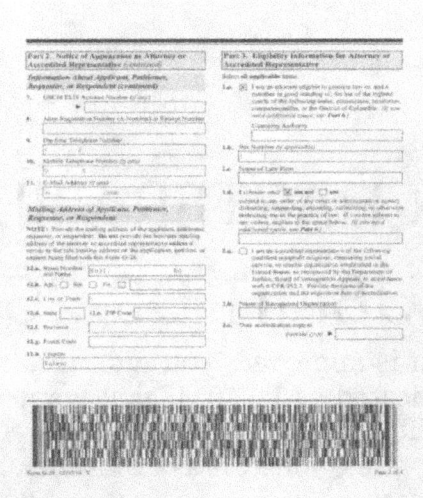

Figure 7-3(b) Form G-28 (2/3)

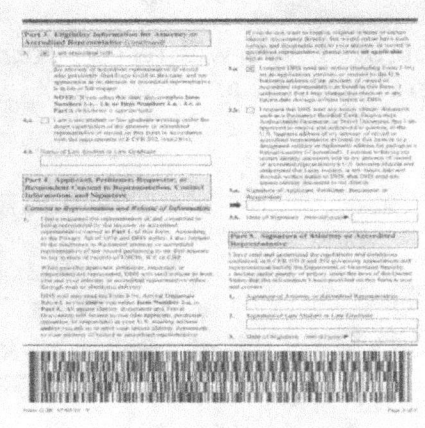

Figure 7-3(c) Form G-28 (3/3)

CHAPTER VIII.
SUBMIT DS-260

If your I-140 petition is approved, you will need to submit Form DS-260. DS-260 is not as complicated as I-140. If you want to save money, you can complete it yourself. I did this myself and will share my personal experience in this chapter. If you prefer, you can ask a lawyer to help you, as they are professionals in this process.

Important: After you submit, you only need to print the confirmation page instead of all the DS-260 pages. Bring that confirmation page to your interview.

1) Form I-797C

When your case is approved, you will receive Form I-797C by email and physical mail, as shown in Figures 8-1 and 8-2.

Figure 8-1(a) I-797C Page 1/2

GET E2/EB2/NIW GREEN CARD FROM ABROAD WITH LOW BUDGET

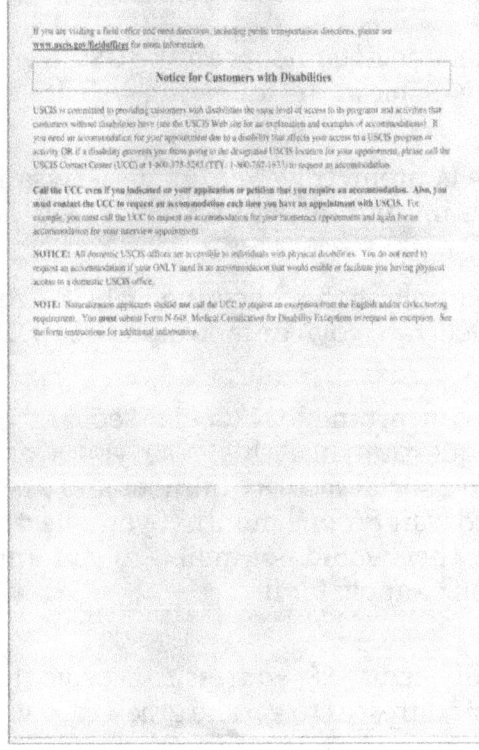

Figure 8-1(b) I-797C Page 2/2

2) Form DS-260

You can find many related documents on the USCIS website. The FAQ related to the DS-260 form is available at the following website.

https://travel.state.gov/content/travel/en/us-visas/visa-information-resources/forms/online-immigrant-visa-forms/ds-260-faqs.html

USCIS provides one sample as the following website. You can learn how to fill that form. https://travel.state.gov/content/dam/visas/DS-260-Exemplar.pdf

As for Figure 8-2(l) concerning SSN (Social Security Number) Information, you will be asked a question like this: "Do you want the Social Security Administration to issue a social security number and a card?" Please select "No" because you will have to wait for one month if you select "Yes". According to my experience and others', they would not mail it to you until you go to the Social Security Administration to apply for it.

In addition, you will need a U.S. address to receive the green card. You may use one of your friends' addresses to get the green card via USPS.

After you finish and submit DS-260, you will see a page like Figure 8-2(n). These are barcodes on the confirmation page. You can bring this page to your interview. Remember that you do not need to print all the DS-260 pages; just print and bring the confirmation page to the consulate.

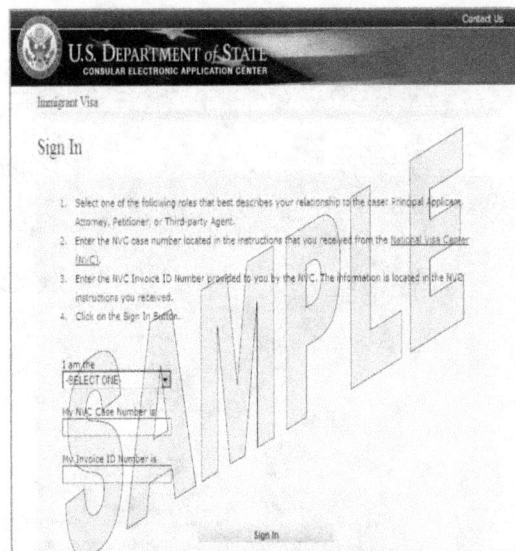

Figure 8-2(a) Sign in

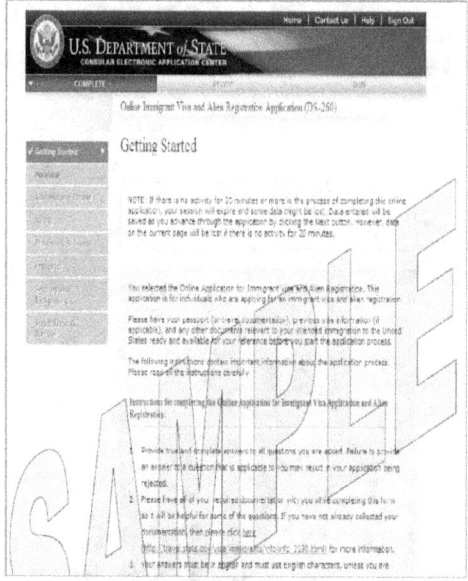

Figure 8-2(b) Getting Started

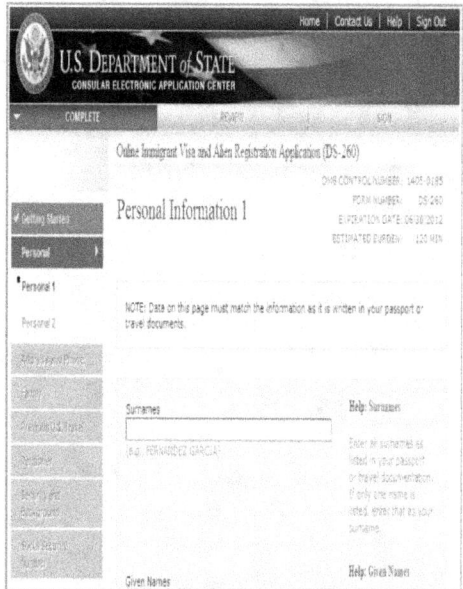

Figure 8-2(c) Personal Info.

Figure 8-2(d) Address Info.

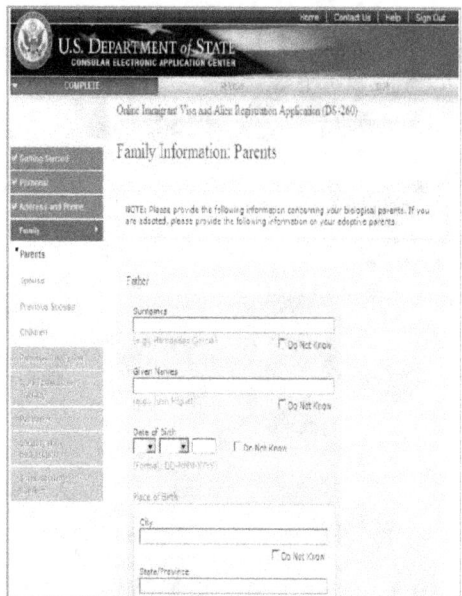

Figure 8-2(e) Personal Info.

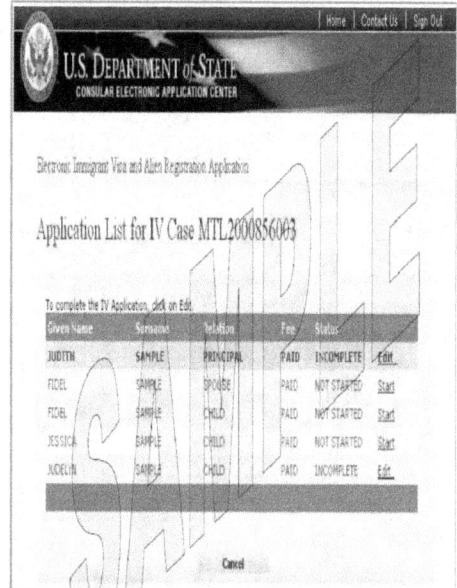

Figure 8-2(f) Address Info.

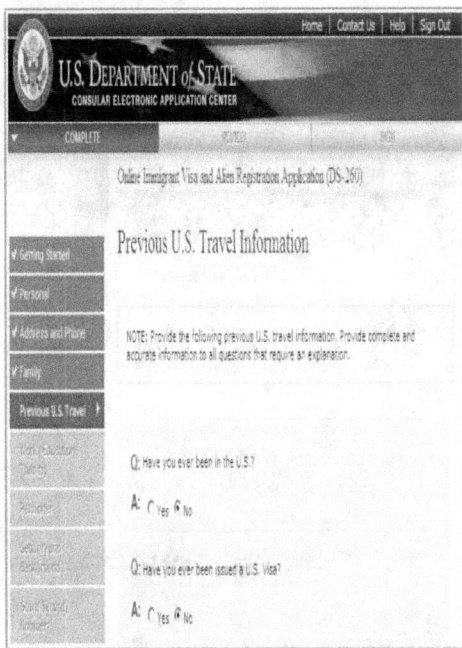

Figure 8-2(g) Travel Info.

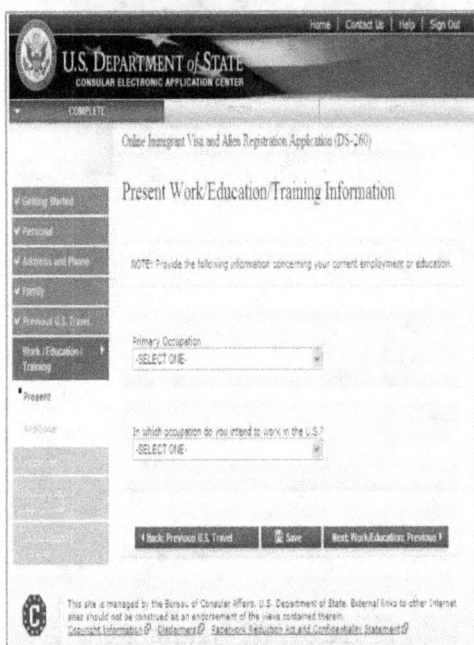

Figure 8-2(h) Work & Education

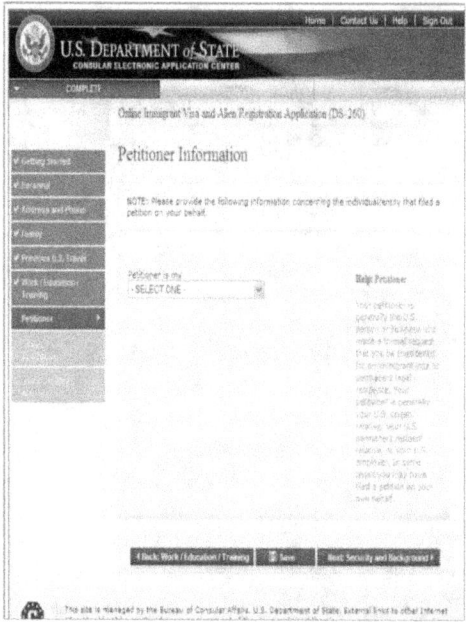

Figure 8-2(i) Petitioner Info.

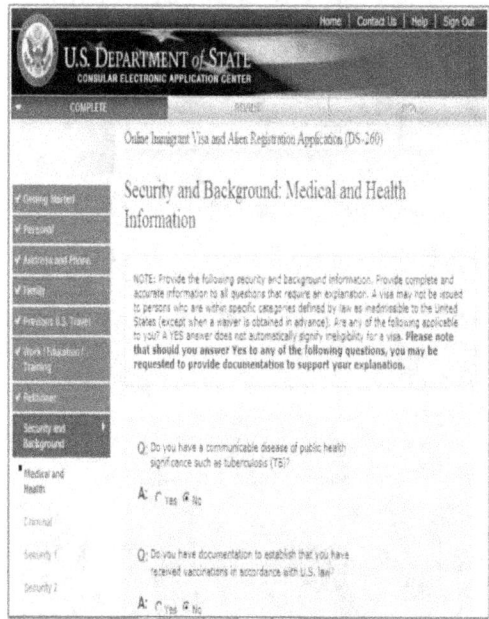

Figure 8-2(j) Health Info.

GET E2/EB2/NIW GREEN CARD FROM ABROAD WITH LOW BUDGET

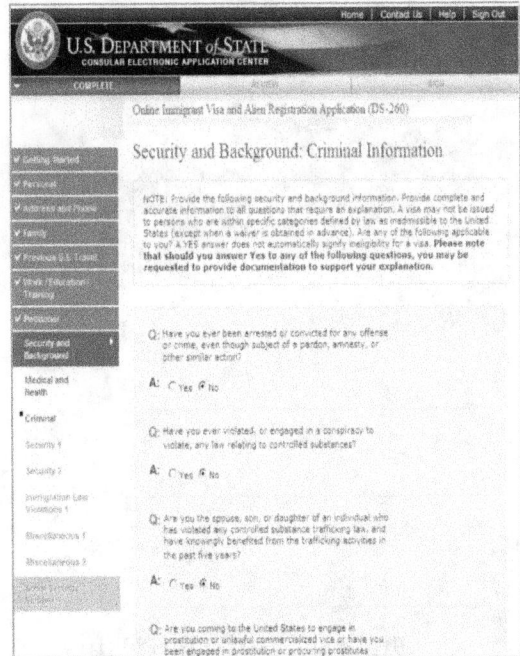

Figure 8-2(k) Security Info.

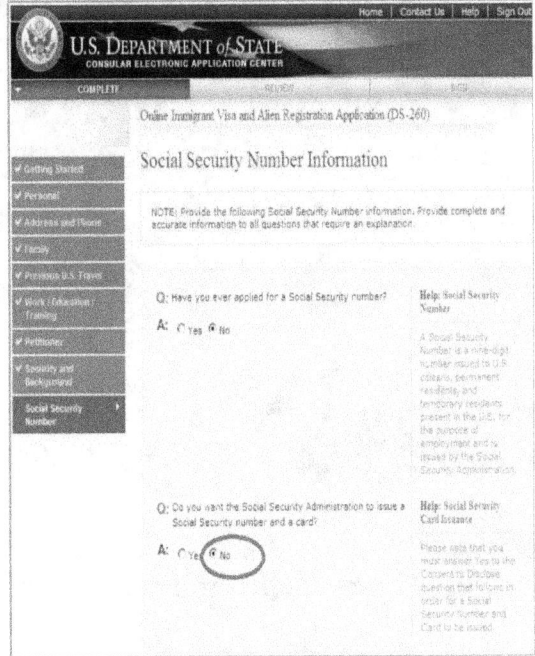

Figure 8-2(l) SSN Info.

Figure 8-2(m) Sign Name

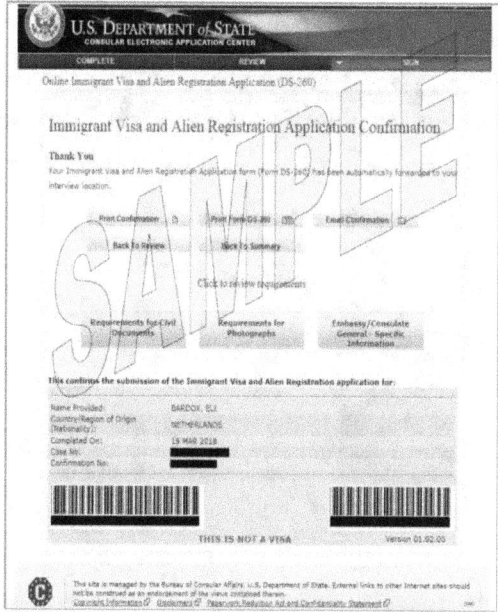

Figure 8-2(n) Finished Result

CHAPTER IX. HEALTH EXAM

Pay attention to the processing time for the health exam at the hospital. In general, it takes 14 days to get the report. Therefore, your interview date should be scheduled more than 14 days after the exam. Otherwise, you should delay your interview. You will also need to bring a photo and your passport. Please refer to Figure 9-1(a).

Additionally, you should go to the designated hospital assigned by the U.S. consulate. If you don't have antibodies for certain diseases, you will need to pay additional fees for vaccinations. Please refer to Figures 9-1(b) and 9-1(c).

After receiving the health exam report, do not open it. It must be submitted unopened to the consulate employee during your interview. If your case is approved by the consulate, you must enter the USA within six months before the health exam expires.

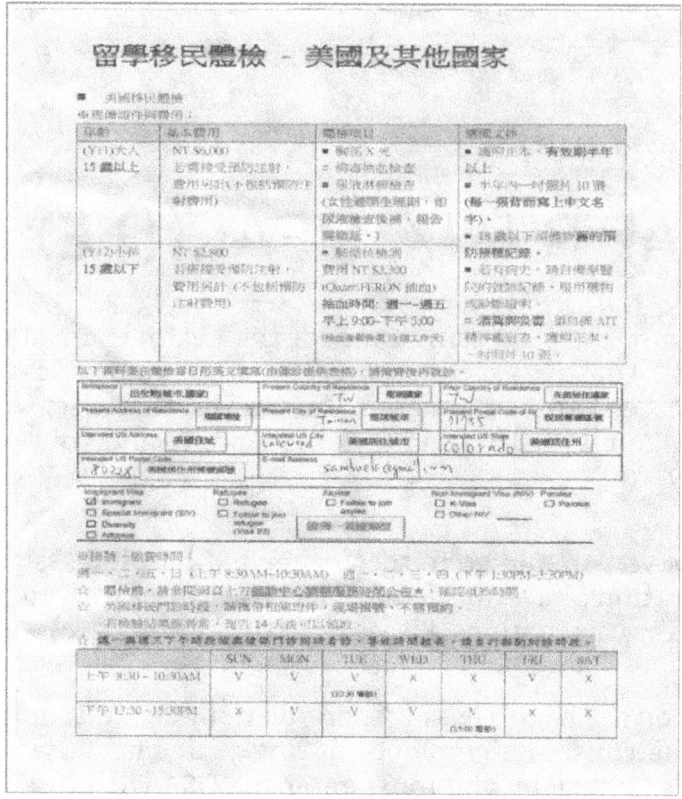

Figure 9-1(a) Health Exam for Immigration Interview

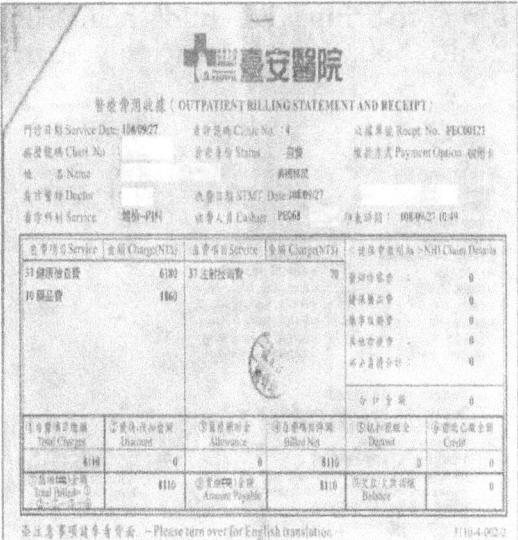

Figure 9-1(b) Health Exam Receipt

Figure 9-1(c) Vaccine Receipt

In addition, don't forget to bring your child's health book to the health exam if you have kids. The health book contains vaccine records, as shown in Figure 9-2.

Figure 9-2(a) Baby Health Book

Figure 9-2(b) Records in Book

CHAPTER X. INTERVIEW

1) Visa Bulletin

After your I-140 petition is approved, you need to check the visa bulletin regularly, as shown in Figures 10-1 and 10-2. You can visit the following website to check the latest information, which is updated monthly. When your status become **current (C)**, they will notify you for a medical examination and interview. Most countries do not have to wait for a long time; however, both China and India have longer waiting periods. The listed date can move forward or backward, so you need to check the bulletin every month. In Figure 10-1, you will find the received and priority dates on the receipt. You need this information to check the visa bulletin.

https://travel.state.gov/content/travel/en/legal/visa-law0/visa-bulletin/2021/visa-bulletin-for-october-2020.html

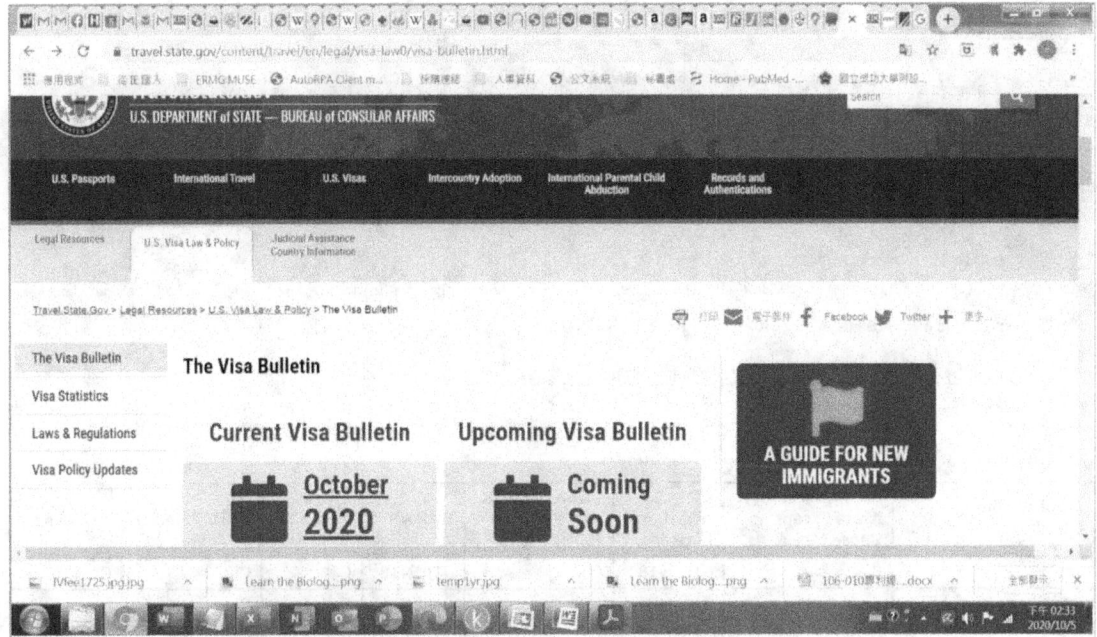

Figure 10-1 The Visa Bulletin on October in 2020.

CHIEN MIN KUO

EMPLOYMENT-BASED PREFERENCES

<u>First</u>: Priority Workers: 28.6% of the worldwide employment-based preference level, plus any numbers not required for fourth and fifth preferences.

<u>Second</u>: Members of the Professions Holding Advanced Degrees or Persons of Exceptional Ability: 28.6% of the worldwide employment-based preference level, plus any numbers not required by first preference.

<u>Third</u>: Skilled Workers, Professionals, and Other Workers: 28.6% of the worldwide level, plus any numbers not required by first and second preferences, not more than 10,000 of which to "*Other Workers".

<u>Fourth</u>: Certain Special Immigrants: 7.1% of the worldwide level.

<u>Fifth</u>: Employment Creation: 7.1% of the worldwide level, not less than 3,000 of which reserved for investors in a targeted rural or high-unemployment area, and 3,000 set aside for investors in regional centers by Sec. 610 of Pub. L. 102-395.

A. FINAL ACTION DATES FOR EMPLOYMENT-BASED PREFERENCE CASES

On the chart below, the listing of a date for any class indicates that the class is oversubscribed (see paragraph 1); "C" means current, i.e., numbers are authorized for issuance to all qualified applicants; and "U" means unauthorized, i.e., numbers are not authorized for issuance. (NOTE: Numbers are authorized for issuance only for applicants whose priority date is **earlier** than the final action date listed below.)

Employment-based	All Chargeability Areas Except Those Listed	CHINA-mainland born	EL SALVADOR GUATEMALA HONDURAS	INDIA	MEXICO	PHILIPPINES	VIETNAM
1st	C	01JUN18	C	01JUN18	C	C	C
2nd	C	01MAR16	C	01SEP09	C	C	C
3rd	C	01JUL17	C	15JAN10	C	C	C
Other Workers	C	01DEC08	C	15JAN10	C	C	C
4th	C	C	01AUG17	C	01SEP18	C	C
Certain Religious Workers	U	U	U	U	U	U	U
5th Non-Regional Center (C5 and T5)	C	15AUG15	C	C	C	C	01AUG17
5th Regional Center (I5 and R5)	U	U	U	U	U	U	U

*Employment Third Preference Other Workers Category: Section 203(e) of the Nicaraguan and Central American Relief Act (NACARA) passed by Congress in November 1997, as amended by Section 1(e) of Pub. L. 105-139, provides that once the Employment Third Preference Other Worker (EW) cut-off date has reached the priority date of the latest EW petition approved prior to November 19, 1997, the 10,000 EW numbers available for a fiscal year are to be reduced by up to 5,000 annually beginning in the following fiscal year. This reduction is to be made for as long as necessary to offset adjustments under the NACARA program. Since the EW final action date reached November 19, 1997 during Fiscal Year 2001, the reduction in the EW annual limit to 5,000 began in Fiscal Year 2002. For Fiscal Year 2021 this reduction will be limited to approximately 150.

B. DATES FOR FILING OF EMPLOYMENT-BASED VISA APPLICATIONS

The chart below reflects dates for filing visa applications within a timeframe justifying immediate action in the application process. Applicants for immigrant visas who have a priority date earlier than the application date in the chart may assemble and submit required documents to the Department of State's National Visa Center, following receipt of notification from the National Visa Center containing detailed instructions. The application date for an oversubscribed category is the priority date of the first applicant who cannot submit documentation to the National Visa Center for an immigrant visa. If a category is designated "current," all applicants in the relevant category may file, regardless of priority date.

The "C" listing indicates that the category is current, and that applications may be filed regardless of the applicant's priority date. The listing of a date for any category indicates that only applicants with a priority date which is earlier than the listed date may file their application.

Visit www.uscis.gov/visabulletininfo for information on whether USCIS has determined that this chart can be used (in lieu of the chart in paragraph 5.A.) this month for filing applications for adjustment of status with USCIS.

Employment-based	All Chargeability Areas Except Those Listed	CHINA-mainland born	EL SALVADOR GUATEMALA HONDURAS	INDIA	MEXICO	PHILIPPINES
1st	C	01SEP20	C	01SEP20	C	C
2nd	C	01OCT16	C	15MAY11	C	C
3rd	C	01JUN18	C	01JAN15	C	C
Other Workers	C	01OCT08	C	01JAN15	C	C
4th	C	C	01FEB18	C	C	C
Certain Religious Workers	C	C	01FEB18	C	C	C
5th Non-Regional Center (C5 and T5)	C	15DEC15	C	C	C	C
5th Regional Center (I5 and R5)	C	15DEC15	C	C	C	C

6. The Department of State has a recorded message with the Final Action date information which can be heard at: (202) 485-7699. This recording is updated on or about the seventeenth of each month with information on final action dates for the following month.

Figure 10-2 The Quota For Employment-Based Preferences.

2) Interview Letter

The interview sample letter is shown in Figure 10-3. It will notify you of when and where you should attend the interview. You can change the schedule if you are not available on that day, but you may have to wait several months for another interview date.

Most officials will use English to ask you questions. However, there is a small chance you could meet an official who speaks your language. After the interview, you will know immediately whether you passed or not. If you pass the interview, they will collect your passport to print the visa stamp on it.

Figure 10-3(a). Interview Letter Envelope

CHIEN MIN KUO

Interview Letter (P4)

September 20, 2019

Dear CHIEN MIN KUO,

The National Visa Center (NVC) is pleased to inform you that we scheduled your immigrant visa interview at the U.S. Embassy or Consulate in TAIPEI, TAIWAN. This interview is for immigrant visa case number filed by CHIEN MIN KUO on behalf of CHIEN MIN KUO. **Please SAVE this letter and bring it to your interview.**

Please promptly read and follow all Interview Preparation Instructions located on the Department of State's web site at: nvc.state.gov/interview. Be sure to review the "Items You Must Bring to Your Visa Interview" checklist prior to traveling to the embassy or consulate.

Important information regarding the required medical appointment is listed on this site. Failure to promptly follow all instructions provided on this site will result in your immigrant visa being refused at the initial interview.

Interview Date and Time

Your immigrant visa interview is at the U.S. Embassy or Consulate in at **08:00 am**. The following applicants should attend this interview:

Name

Petitioners are not required -- and at some locations, may not be allowed -- to attend the applicant's visa interview.

What to Do if You Cannot Keep the Interview

Some Embassies/Consulates reschedule interview appointments themselves; others utilize an outside service provider to reschedule appointments. To determine the proper procedure for rescheduling your interview

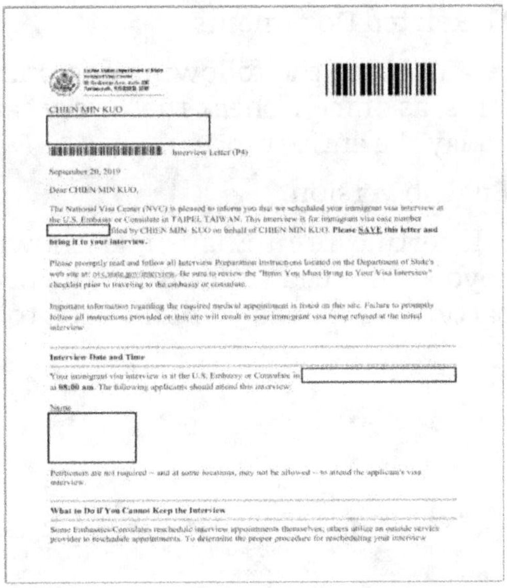

Figure 10-3(b). Interview Letter 1/2

Preparing for Your Visa Interview

All eligible applicants must complete the following tasks before their visa interview. Detailed instructions for each step are online at nvc.state.gov/interview (English) and nvc.state.gov/interview/Espanol (Spanish).

1. Bring this letter to your medical examination because the panel physician may need to review it before performing the examination.
2. To determine the proper procedure for your medical appointment, please go to the Department of State's web site at: nvc.state.gov/interview. Under "Step 2," select your interview location from the dropdown, click "Download PDF," and follow your Embassy/Consulate's instructions.
3. If a sponsor filed an I-864 (Affidavit of Support) AND provided NVC with proof of an IRS Federal Income Tax Extension in lieu of a Federal Income Tax Return, you must bring the sponsor's most recent Federal Income Tax Return to the visa interview.
4. You must bring to the interview original versions of all civil documents and certificates submitted to NVC. You may need to get updated financial documents and police certificates. Failure to present all necessary documents to the Consular Officer will result in your immigrant visa being refused at the initial interview.

You can also watch a video at nvc.state.gov/resources. This instructional video is available in eight languages.

Family Reunification Parole (FRP) Program Interviews

If you are participating in the Cuban Family Reunification Parole Program, view the program website at havana.usembassy.gov/cfrp.html (English) or spanish.havana.usembassy.gov/cfrp.html (Spanish) and follow the instructions.

- If you are participating in the Haitian Family Reunification Parole Program, view the website at uscis.gov/hfrp.

Did you read the U.S. embassy or consulate's interview instructions on nvc.state.gov/interview to learn:

- The approved medical facilities where you can get a medical examination
- Whether you are required to register for a passport courier service prior to the interview
- Security requirements for entering the U.S. Embassy
- If there are any forms or documents **not** listed above that the embassy wants you to bring to the interview
- Whether you are required to provide the above documents to the embassy **prior** to your interview

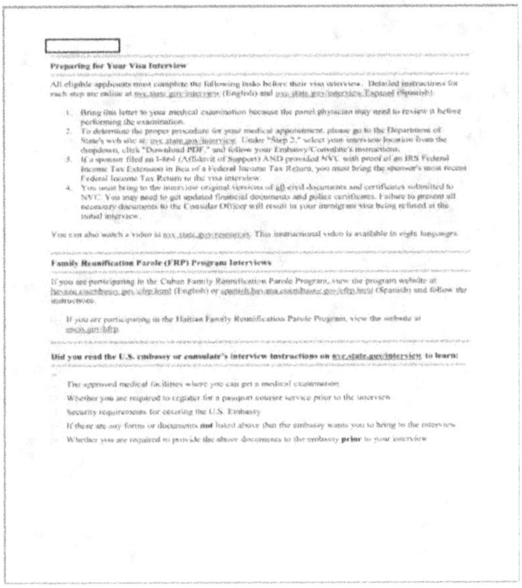

Figure 10-3(c). Interview Letter 2/2

3) Prepare and Bring All Related Documents

You need to prepare and bring the following documents to your interview. Pay close attention to this, as officers check these very carefully. Missing any of these documents will delay the entire process.

a) Birth Certificate in English version.

If you have the birth certificate in English, as shown in Figure 10-4, that would be great. If not, you will need to translate the original one and have it notarized by a third party. This means you will need to spend more time and money.

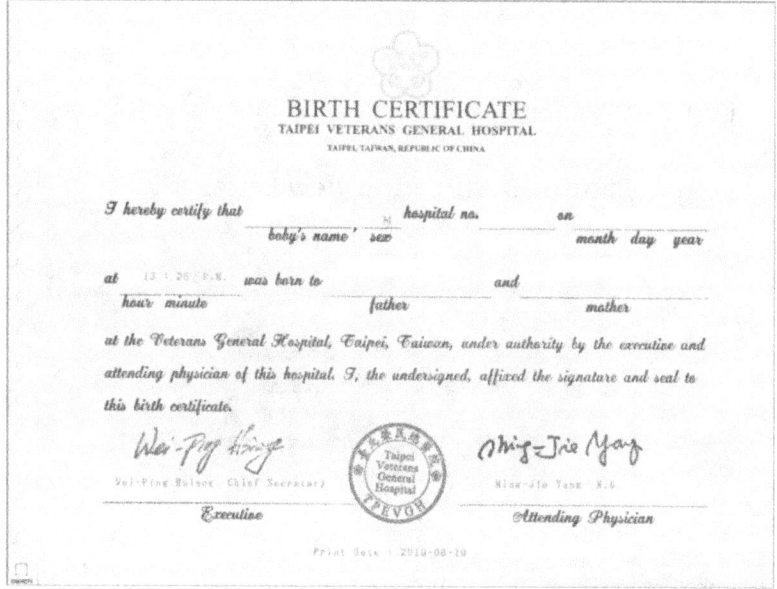

Figure 10-4 Birth Certificate in English Version

b) Two Photos with 2*2 Inch within Six Months.

You should prepare two photos, 2x2 inches in size, taken within the past six months. Detailed format requirements can be found at the following website:

https://travel.state.gov/content/travel/en/us-visas/visa-information-resources/photos/photo-examples.html

If the photo on your passport was taken within the last six months, you can use the same photo to save some money.

c) Valid Passport

You should prepare your latest and old passports that contain U.S.A. visas with entry and exit stamps. **Important:** the expiration date of your current passport must be more than six months from now.

d) I-140 Approval Notice

You can prepare the I-140 approval notice as Figure 10-5 too. But I think they would not check this because they have this document before you attend the interview. However, it is better to prepare all documents. You may go to the second interview if you don't bring all documents. I saw two men who miss some documents so that they have a long talk with the document reviewer.

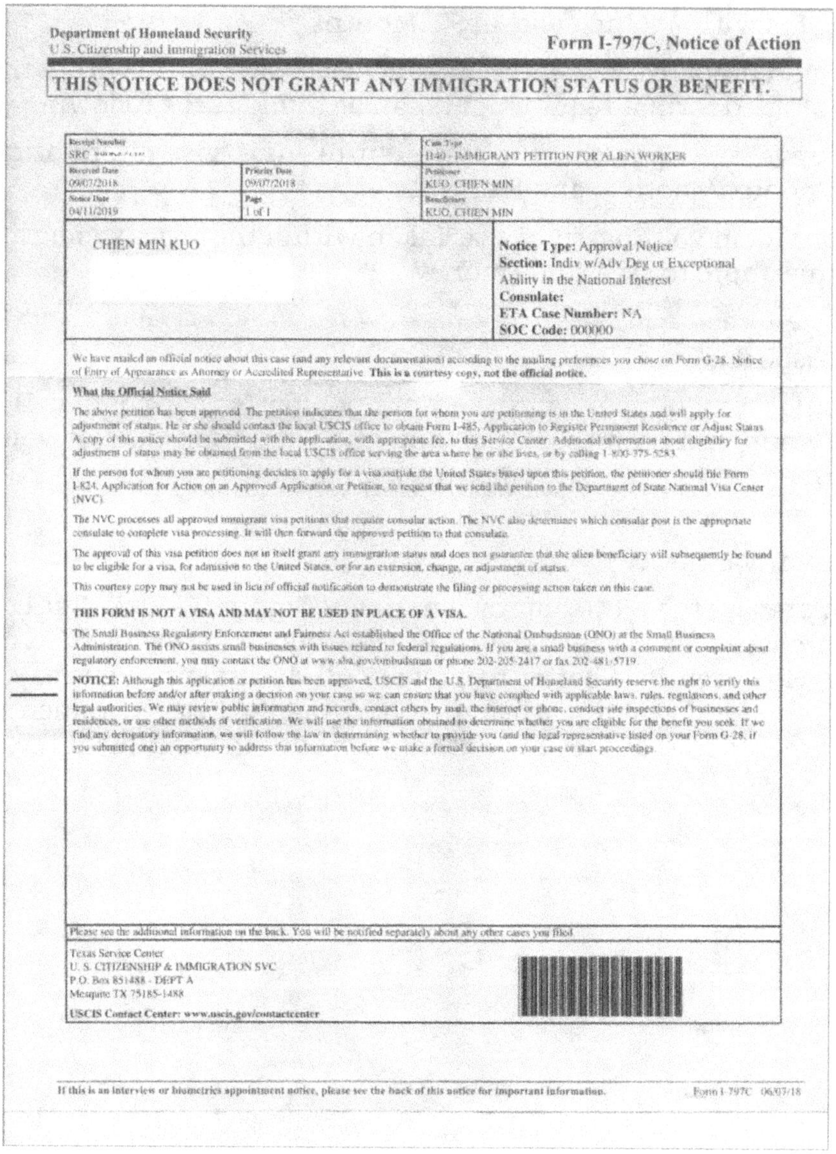

Figure 10-5 I-140 Approval Notice

e) Evidence that you are a non-immigrant

You can provide the visa stamps, I-20s, I-797 approval notices, and so on.

f) Tax transcripts of the last three years

If you live outside the United States, you do not need to prepare this. However, if you live in the United States, you will need to prepare these tax transcripts.

g) Household registration transcript issued by local government

Definitely, you must prepare the household registration transcript in English, as shown in Figure 10-6. It must be issued by the local government. You cannot provide only a copy version; the reviewer requires it to have a stamp.. **They do not accept the copy version alone.** You should prepare **both** the original and copy versions.

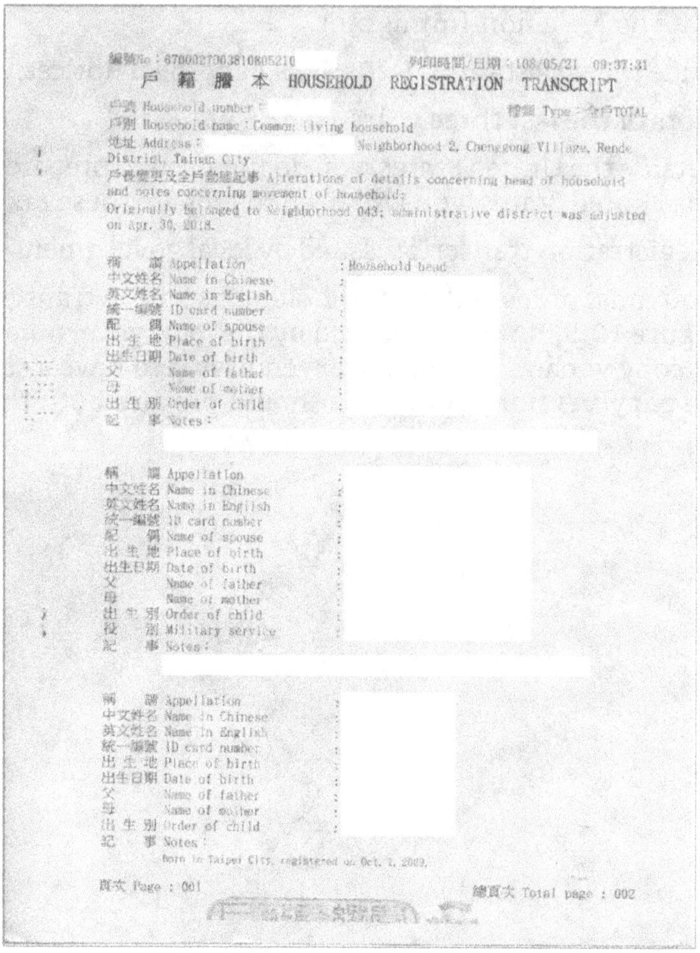

編號No：670002T063810805210　　　　列印時間/日期：108/05/21　09:37:31

戶　籍　謄　本 HOUSEHOLD REGISTRATION TRANSCRIPT

戶號 Household number：　　　　　　　　類別 Type：全戶TOTAL

戶別 Household name：Common living household

地址 Address：　　　　Neighborhood 2, Chenggong Village, Rende District, Tainan City

戶長變更及全戶動態記事 Alterations of details concerning head of household and notes concerning movement of household:

Originally belonged to Neighborhood 043; administrative district was adjusted on Apr. 30, 2018.

稱　　謂 Appellation　　　　：Household head
中文姓名 Name in Chinese　　：
英文姓名 Name in English　　：
統一編號 ID card number　　：
配　　偶 Name of spouse　　：
出 生 地 Place of birth　　：
出生日期 Date of birth　　：
父　　　 Name of father　　：
母　　　 Name of mother　　：
出 生 別 Order of child　　：
記　　事 Notes：

稱　　謂 Appellation　　　　：
中文姓名 Name in Chinese　　：
英文姓名 Name in English　　：
統一編號 ID card number　　：
配　　偶 Name of spouse　　：
出 生 地 Place of birth　　：
出生日期 Date of birth　　：
父　　　 Name of father　　：
母　　　 Name of mother　　：
出 生 別 Order of child　　：
役　　別 Military service　　：
記　　事 Notes：

稱　　謂 Appellation　　　　：
中文姓名 Name in Chinese　　：
英文姓名 Name in English　　：
統一編號 ID card number　　：
出 生 地 Place of birth　　：
出生日期 Date of birth　　：
父　　　 Name of father　　：
母　　　 Name of mother　　：
出 生 別 Order of child　　：
記　　事 Notes：
Born in Taipei City, registered on Oct. 1, 2009.

頁次 Page：001　　　　總頁次 Total page：002

Figure 10-6 Household Registration Transcript

h) Medical examination and vaccination record

Most adults do not have vaccination records, as shown in Figure 10-7. Therefore, their antibodies will be checked. For children, you need to prepare the vaccination records, which will be used when they attend the medical exams.

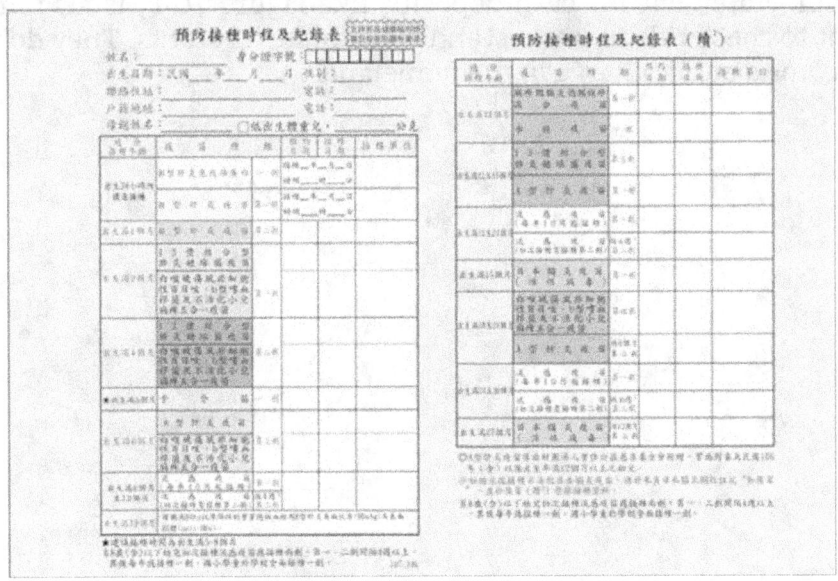

Figure 10-7 Vaccination Record

i) Diploma

You should prepare all your diplomas, including bachelor's, master's, Ph.D., equivalency evaluations, and transcripts. It's better to make a checklist to avoid missing any documents.

j) Official bank statement

Your bank statement for cash deposits, like Figure 10-8, is also important. They want to check this to understand your financial status. They do not want you to become a public charge in the homeland.

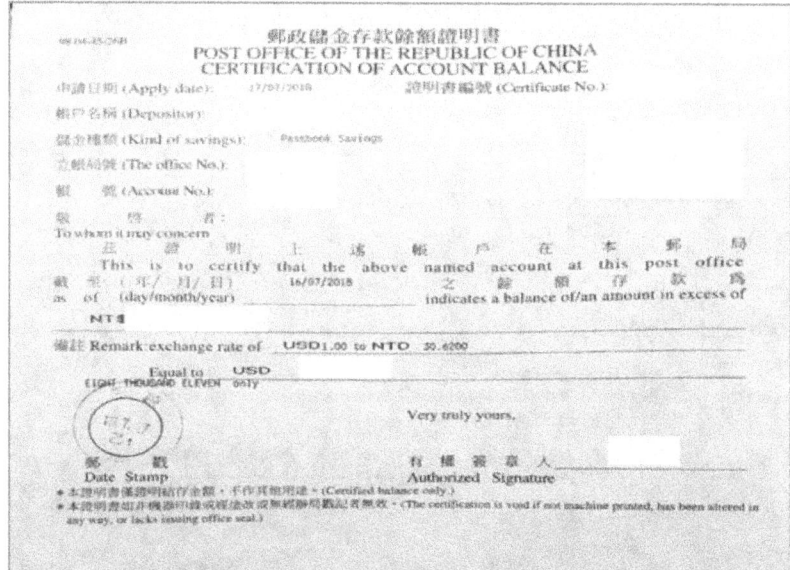

Figure 10-8 Bank Statement

k) Marriage/Divorce certificate

You should prepare the marriage/divorce certificate if applicable. Please refer to Figure 10-9 for a sample. This certificate allows your spouse to gain the green card with you at the same time. If you married your spouse recently, they will ask you many questions due to concerns about fraud. However, if you have been married for many years, this should not be a problem.

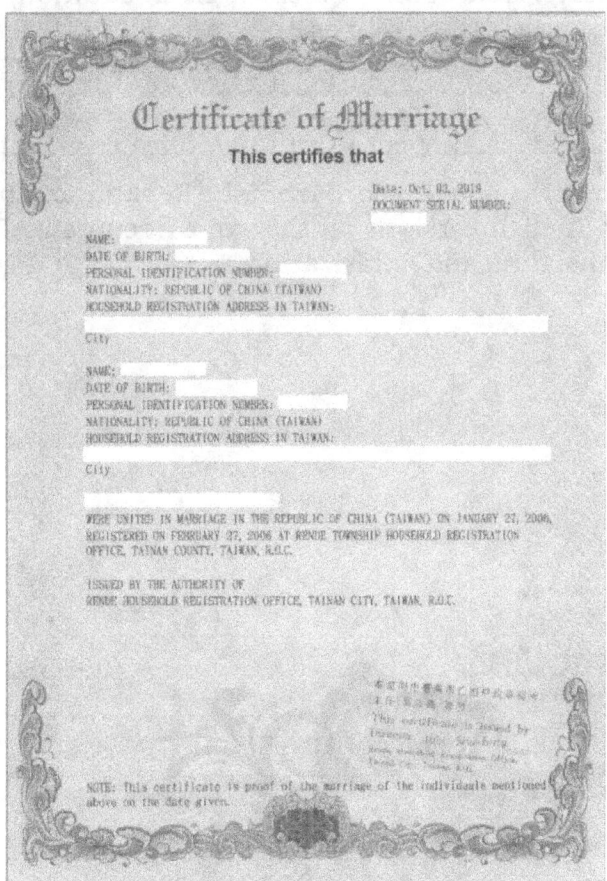

Figure 10-9 Marriage Certificate

l) Police criminal record certificate

If you have lived in different countries for more than 6 months, you should prepare all the necessary police certificates. These certificates are only valid for one year.

Figure 10-10 shows the police certificate from the United Kingdom. If you have lived in the United Kingdom, you can visit the following website to apply for a police certificate: ACRO Police Certificates. In addition, they will ask you to provide an electronic utility bill, as shown in Figure 10-11, to verify your current address. Therefore, you need to apply for an electronic utility bill in English.

https://www.acro.police.uk/s/acro-services/police-certificates

Figure 10-12 shows the police record from the Republic of China. They provide both Chinese and English versions on the same document. This way, you will save money on translation and notarization.

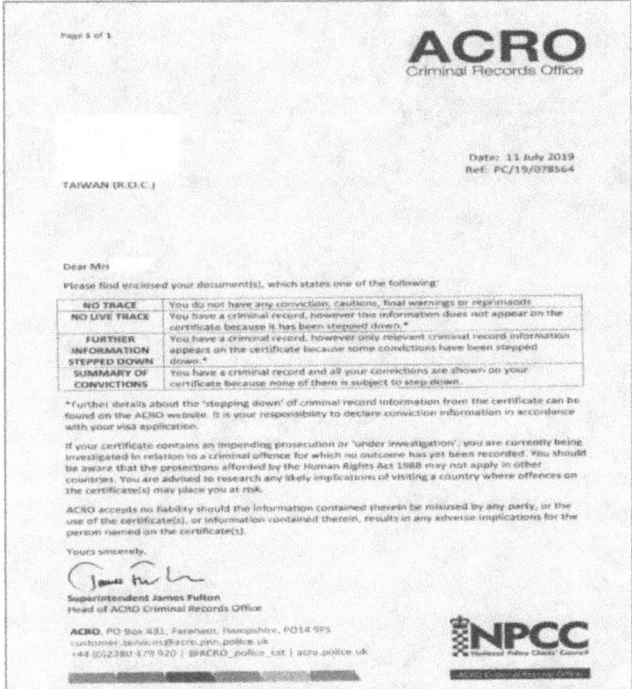

Figure 10-10(a) U.K. Police Certificate Note

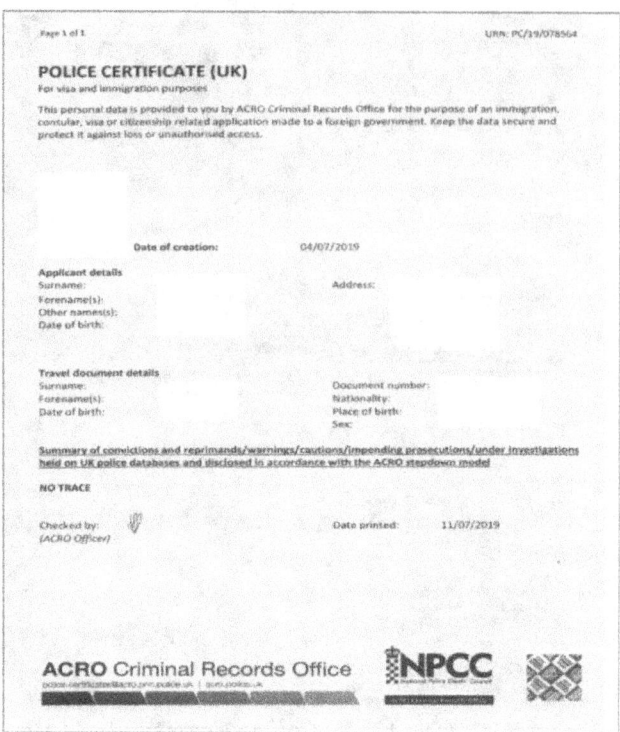

Figure 10-10(b) U.K. Police Certificate

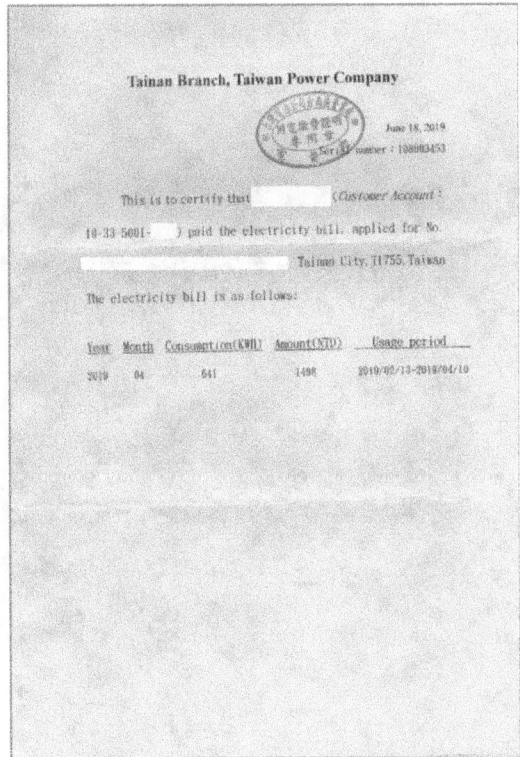

Figure 10-11 Electricity Bill

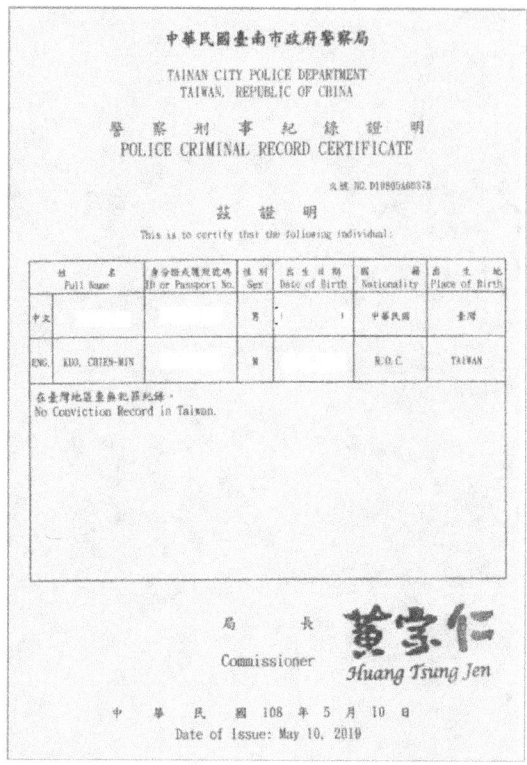

Figure 10-12 TW Police Certificate

GET E2/EB2/NIW GREEN CARD FROM ABROAD WITH LOW BUDGET

m) Court verdict

A court verdict will be required, if applicable. Criminal records should also be disclosed in DS-260. This is critical to homeland security.

n) Military service discharge orders

You can prepare the military service discharge orders as shown in Figure 10-13. All the documents must be in English. I translated mine myself, as shown in Figure 10-14. If you are from R.O.C., you can use this sample to modify. Every translated document should be notarized without exception. Please refer to Figure 10-15.

Figure 10-13(a) Military Service Discharge Orders (Front)

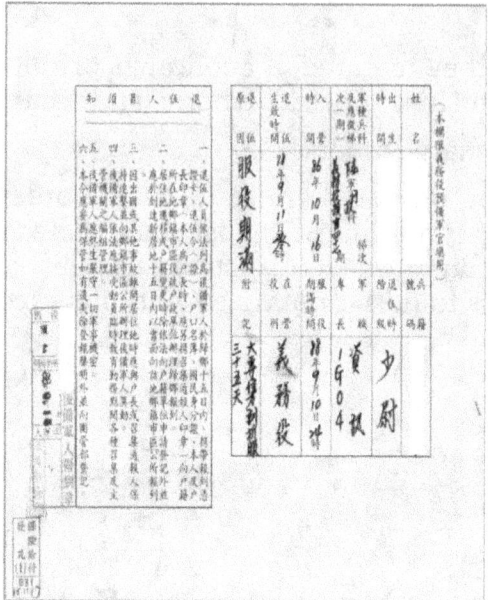

Figure 10-13(b) Military Service Discharge Orders (Back)

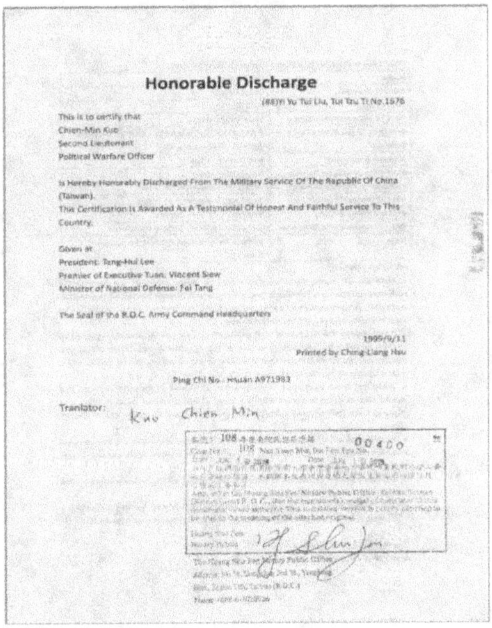

Honorable Discharge

(88)Yi Yu Tui Liu, Tui Tzu Ti No.1576

This is to certify that
Chien-Min Kuo
Second Lieutenant
Political Warfare Officer

Is Hereby Honorably Discharged From The Military Service Of The Republic Of China (Taiwan).
This Certification Is Awarded As A Testimonial Of Honest And Faithful Service To This Country.

Given at
President: Teng-Hui Lee
Premier of Executive Yuan: Vincent Siew
Minister of National Defense: Fei Tang

The Seal of the R.O.C. Army Command Headquarters

1999/9/11
Printed by Ching-Liang Hsu

Ping Chi No.: Hsuan A971983

Tranlator: Kuo Chien Min

00400

Figure 10-14 Military Service Discharge Orders in English Version (Front)

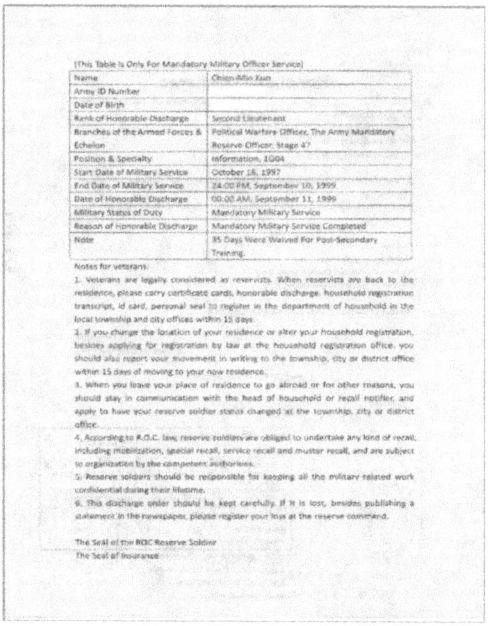

(This Table Is Only For Mandatory Military Officer Service)

Name	Chien-Min Kuo
Army ID Number	
Date of Birth	
Rank of Honorable Discharge	Second Lieutenant
Branches of the Armed Forces & Echelon	Political Warfare Officer, The Army Mandatory Reserve Officer, Stage 47
Position & Specialty	Information, 1004
Start Date of Military Service	October 16, 1997
End Date of Military Service	24:00 PM, September 10, 1999
Date of Honorable Discharge	00:00 AM, September 11, 1999
Military Status of Duty	Mandatory Military Service
Reason of Honorable Discharge	Mandatory Military Service Completed
Note	35 Days Were Waived For Post-Secondary Training.

Notes for veterans:

1. Veterans are legally considered as reservists. When reservists are back to the residence, please carry certificate cards, honorable discharge, household registration transcript, id card, personal seal to register in the department of household in the local township and city offices within 15 days.
2. If you change the location of your residence or alter your household registration, besides applying for registration by law at the household registration office, you should also report your movement in writing to the township, city or district office within 15 days of moving to your new residence.
3. When you leave your place of residence to go abroad or for other reasons, you should stay in communication with the head of household or recall notifier, and apply to have your reserve soldier status changed at the township, city or district office.
4. According to R.O.C. law, reserve soldiers are obliged to undertake any kind of recall, including mobilization, special recall, service recall and muster recall, and are subject to organization by the competent authorities.
5. Reserve soldiers should be responsible for keeping all the military related work confidential during their lifetime.
6. This discharge order should be kept carefully. If it is lost, besides publishing a statement in the newspaper, please register your loss at the reserve command.

The Seal of the ROC Reserve Soldier
The Seal of Insurance

Figure 10-14 Military Service Discharge Orders in English Version (Back)

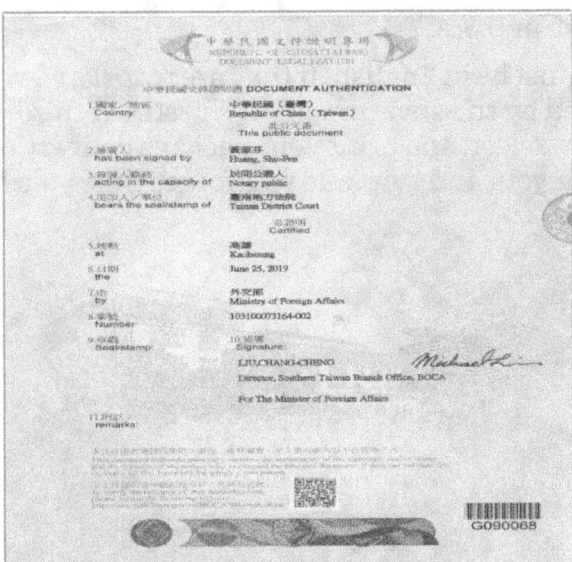

Figure 10-15 Military Service Discharge Orders Notarized by Government

o) Future plan to live in U.S.A.

All documents must be in English. If they are translated versions, you need to have them notarized by the government or a certified third party. Additionally, you need to register, select, and print your package delivery options as shown in Figure 10-16 before your interview. If you forget this, your interview could be canceled.

Future Research Plans

In the coming years, I intend to extend my research on computer-aided bibliometrics methodology, text mining and legal information system. Particular challenges in the field of bibliometrics was to design new useful evaluation index, visualization tools, journal information retrieval, open access journal solution and so on. In my future work, I intend to extend my prior experiments and innovation to cover additional scientific literature bibliometrics system and computer added-value legal system.

methodology innovation, publication, red dot award, international product, international cooperation

1. Apply Artificial Intelligence Technology to Journal Manuscript Submission Decision Support System

One area I would like to extend my research on is the integration of artificial intelligence methodology with journal article submission decision support system. Owing to the past experiences, many people are interested in my journal manuscript submission decision support system including Elsevier Ltd, IEEE, Edanz Group Ltd and so on. Therefore, I plan to do more researches on this subject. The ontology in artificial intelligence (AI) would be a good direction to enhance the system. Currently, I am cooperating with NCKU professor to apply ontology methodology on patent information retrieval system now. In the future, I intend to transfer my previous relation database to owl and ontology. Redefine the schema with RDF and use JENA API to integrate with my previous ASP.net codes. RDF Query Language SPARQL would be used to replace SQL to proceed with intelligent query. This would make system more useful and easy to use. Advance publication, patent and product could be extended.

2. The add-valued system to search results from academic journal search engine and information retrieval

Most search engines or information retrieval systems are focus on generating search results from end user's the input terms or inquiry condition. I plan to develop more advanced add-valued analysis or usage from general search results. There are several potential applications including 1)Looking forward research intelligence and latest hot research subjects analysis method and system, 2)Professional field dictionary with computer aided vocabulary collection and generation, 3)Original, milestone and pioneer articles filter and recommend system, 4)Outstanding and pioneer scholars filter and recommend system. There are still many other innovation methods and systems can be explored and integrated with traditional search engine to provide more rich and variable information for end users.

3. The legal information management and application method and system

Compared with other fields, there are very few information science scholars or computer scientist who do the research or develop new system in the field of legal. The journal publication, patent and software related to the legal information system are seldom in the past. I have several publications and patents in the legal subject area were published before. They are as the following: 1)The law office and lawyer recommendation method and system (one master thesis, one conference paper and one patent), 2)The drug sentencing decision support system(one patent, one conference paper), 3)The intellectual property sentence calculator (one master thesis, one conference paper and one patent), 4)Legal document computer-aided generation method and system (one patent). There are still many interesting subjects I want to proceed with research and development such as: parole threshold decision support system, assigned to prison decision support system, the state compensation of miscarriage of justice calculator, the immigration case information management system and so on.

Figure 10-16 Future Plan Proposal.

p) Form DS-260

After you submit Form DS-260 online, you only need to print the confirmation page instead of all the DS-260 pages. Bring that confirmation page, as shown in Figure 10-17, to your interview. After you submit DS-260, you cannot edit it anymore. However, you can ask the official to edit it again when you attend the interview. You can also call the consulate before your interview to have the system unlocked so you can modify it again. I discovered this when I found an error after I submitted it.

https://travel.state.gov/content/dam/visas/DS-260-Exemplar.pdf

Figure 10-17 DS-260 Confirmation Page

q) Yellow packet

You are required to register the package delivery online before you attend the interview, as shown in Figure 10-18. After you register, you should print your confirmation (Figure 10-19) and bring it to the interview.

If you are approved after the interview, they will mail you an approval notice (Figure 10-20) and a yellow package (Figure 10-21). Each member of your family will receive a yellow package. You are not allowed to open it (Figure 10-22). When you travel by airplane, do not put it in your checked luggage. You should carry it in your hand-held luggage. When you pass through customs, you should give it to the customs officer. It is better to go through a large airport rather than a small one, as customs officers at large airports have more experience dealing with this. Therefore, please try to land at a large airport, such as LAX, SFO, and so on.

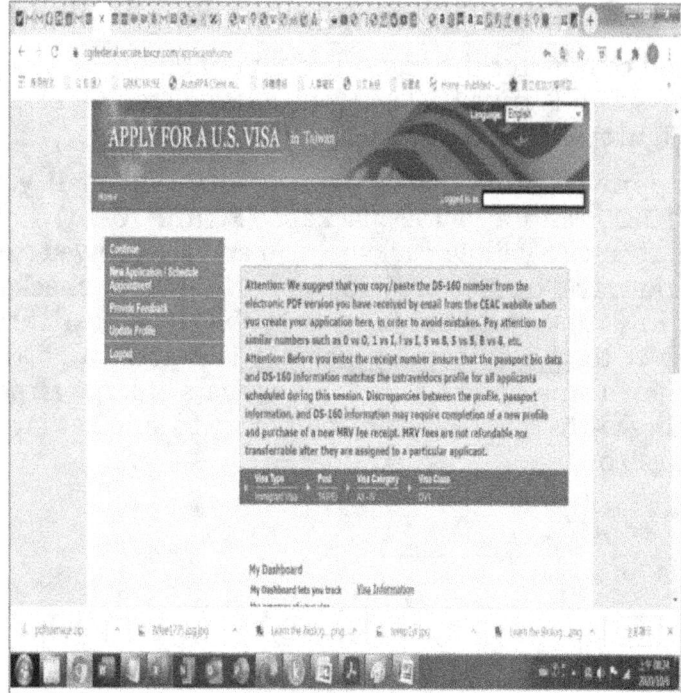

Figure 10-18 Package Delivery

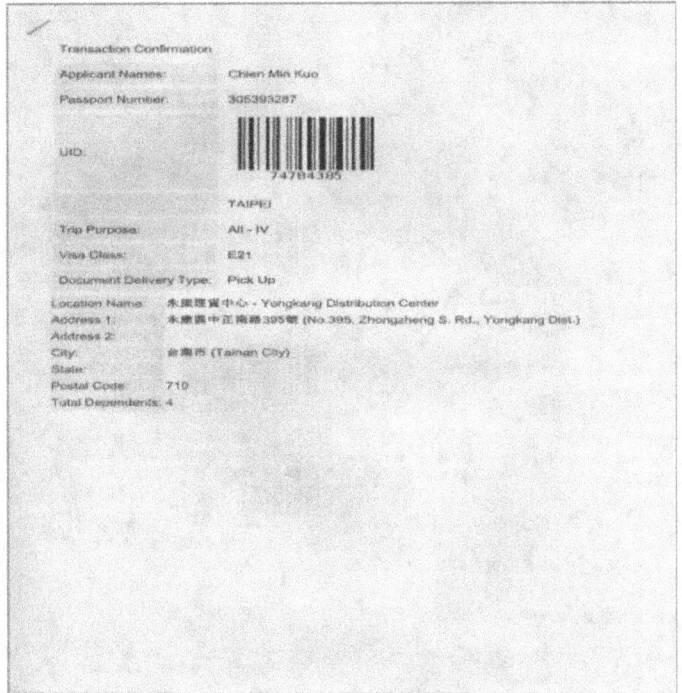

Figure 10-19 Delivery Confirmation

Dear applicant,

Congratulations on the approval of your immigrant visa.

This notice is to remind you that you will not receive a sealed package of documents because your immigrant visa was issued under the paperless Modernized Immigrant Visa Program process. You immigrant visa will be endorsed with a "IV Docs in CCD" annotation, which means that documents previously hand carried by the immigrant are now automatically forwarded to the DHS official at the port of entry.

In some cases, immigrants will receive an immigrant visa with two annotations. If your visa has a second annotation saying "CLASS A or B req. ATTN of USPHS at POE", you will receive a sealed medical package. You must carry this packet with you to the United States.

申請者您好：

在此告知您的移民簽證已核准。

由於您的簽證是以最新的電子化系統來核發，此信是為了提醒您，您將不會收到簽證包裹。美國移民簽證辦事處會在您的護照簽證內附註 "IV DOCS in CCD" 表示您先前所寄來的個人文件皆已經由電子化系統傳送到美國海關及邊境保護局(CBP)。

至於少部分的申請文件，則會有第二項備註。若您的簽證有第二項 "CLASS A or B req. ATTN of USPHS at POE" 此備註，意思是您將會收到您的體檢報告。您則需要帶著此體檢報告（不可拆封）並且攜帶入美國海關。

謝謝您

Figure 10-20 Approval Notice

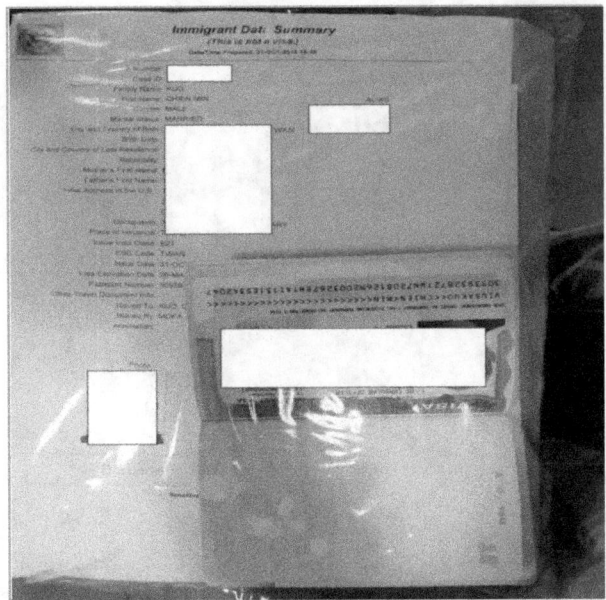

Figure 10-21 Yellow Packet

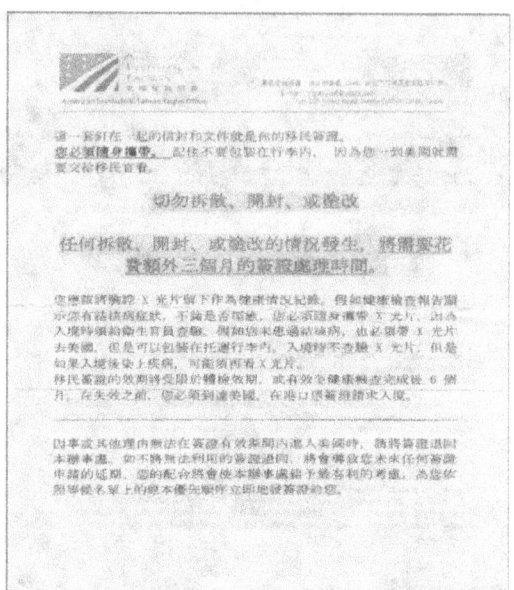

Figure 10-22(a) Yellow Packet Reminder in Chinese

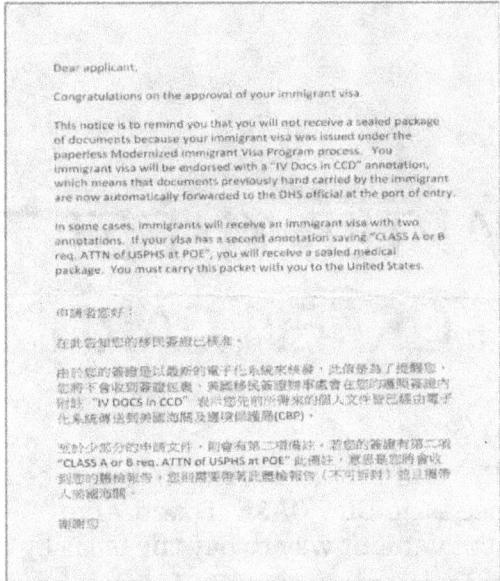

Figure 10-22(b) Yellow Packet Reminder in English

CHAPTER XI. GET THE GREEN CARD

1) Pay the Fee for Green Card

In Figure 11-1, USCIS will provide you with a notice on how to pay for the green card. You will need the DOS CASE ID and Alien Registration Number to pay the bill. The most convenient way to pay the fee is by credit card.

After you pay the fee online, you will receive a confirmation page, as shown in Figure 11-2. It's okay if you don't print it, as customs officers will not check this. After landing in the United States, you will need to wait one to four months to receive the green card. If you don't plan to stay for a long time, you can return to your country. When the green card is mailed to your provided address, you can ask a friend to mail the green card to your country.

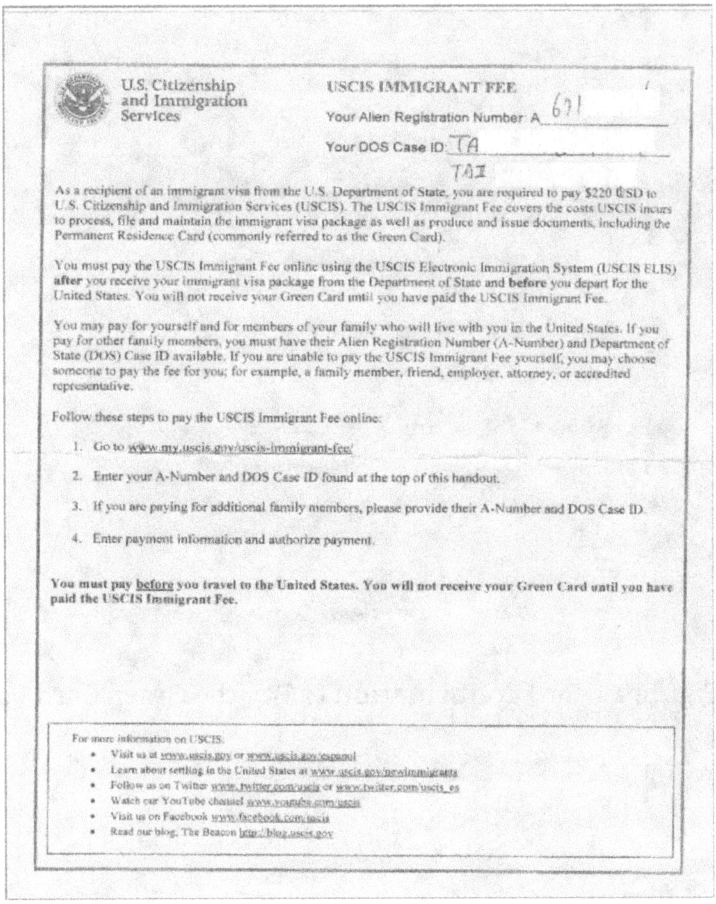

GET E2/EB2/NIW GREEN CARD FROM ABROAD WITH LOW BUDGET

Figure 11-1 Pay the Green Card Notice

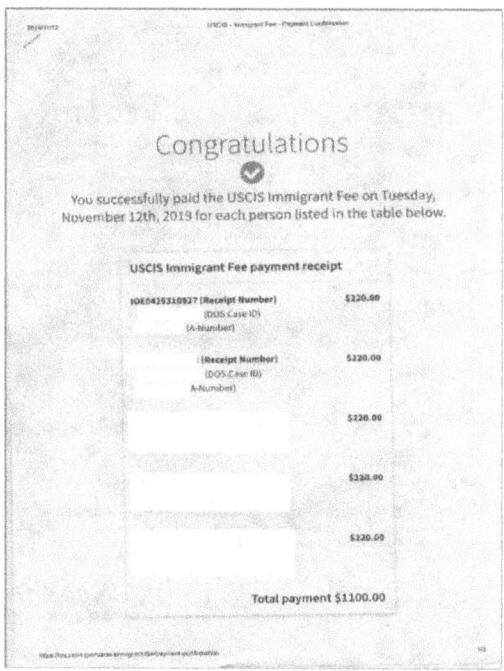

Figure 11-2(a) Confirmation to Pay the Green Card ½

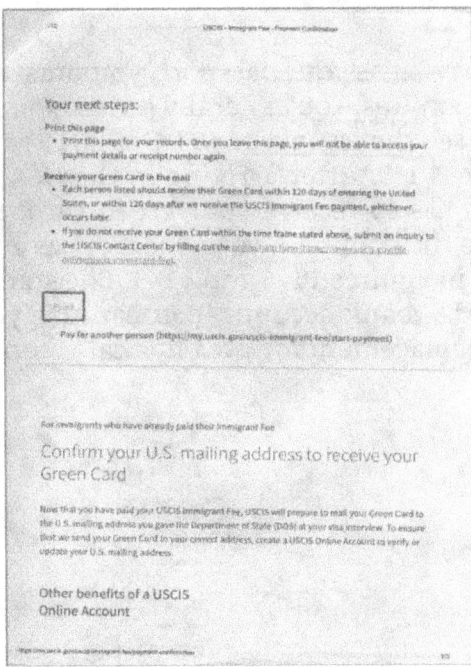

Figure 11-2(b) Confirmation to Pay the Green Card 2/2

2) Travel

When the consulate returns your passport, you must enter the United States before the health exam expires. You generally have six months before the health exam expires. You can see the issue date (31 Oct 2019) and the expiration date (26 Mar 2020) in Figure 11-3. After arriving in the USA, you will need to wait about two to four months to receive your green card. Before you receive the green card, you can use the stamp on your passport as a temporary Form I-551 (Green card), as shown in Figures 11-4 and 11-5. The stamp is valid for one year. When applying for a U.S. bank account, you can use your passport with the stamp as a temporary replacement for the physical green card.

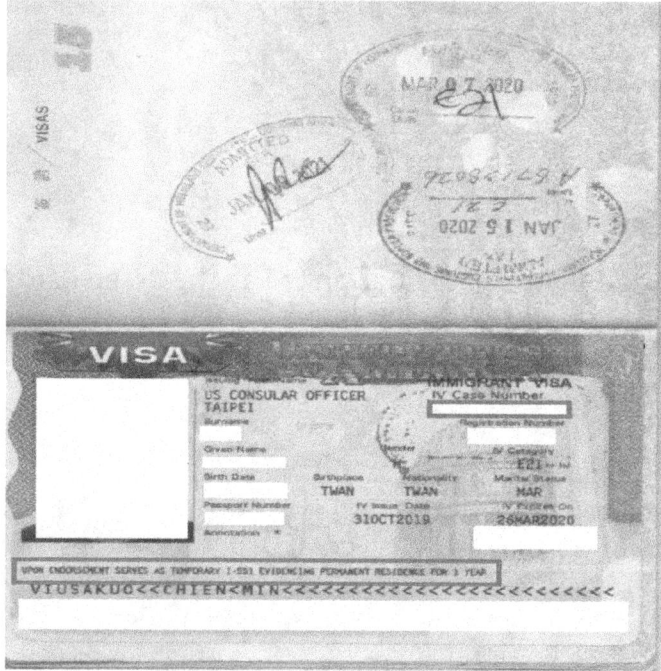

Figure 11-3 Temporary VISA before Green Card

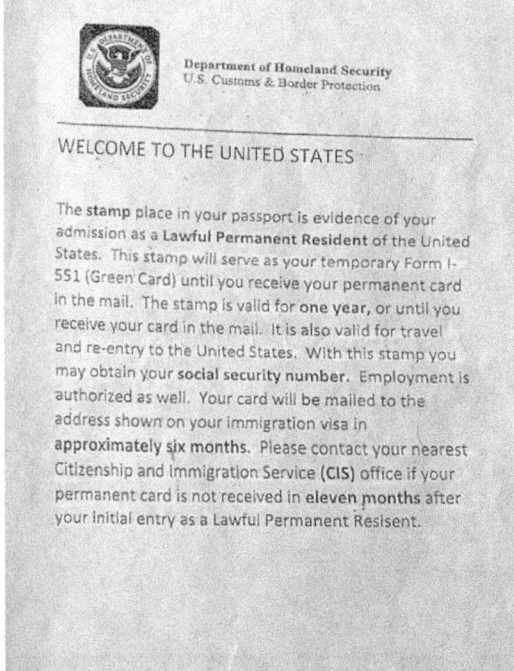

Figure 11-4 Form I-551 Notice

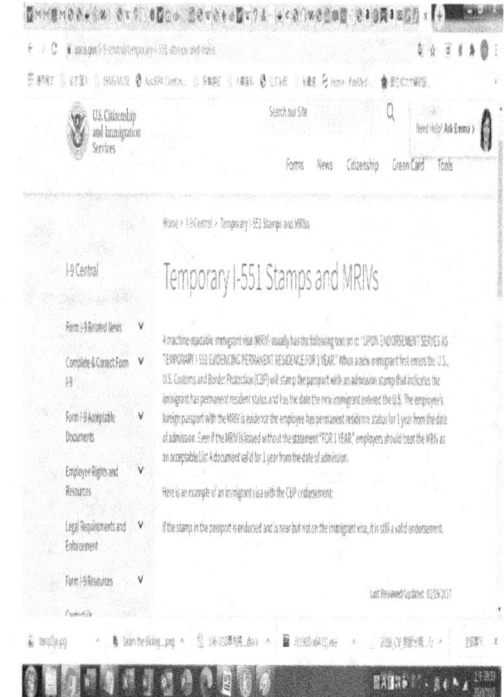

Figure 11-5 Form I-551 Stamps and MRIVs

3) Receive the Green Card

A sample of a "permanent resident card" (often called a 'green card') of the United States (2021) is illustrated in Figure 11-6 (Wikipedia, 2021). After you receive the green card, you can use it to replace the visa in your passport.

Figure 11-6 Sample of Green Card

CHAPTER XII. APPENDIX

If you want to save money on printing your visa photo, you can try this free software. It is totally free and powerful. One highly cited free software is "Photocap." Please refer to Figure A-1. It has both English and Chinese versions. You can download it from the following two websites.

1)https://agenda2918.pixnet.net/blog/post/284983508-photocap-6.0-%E6%AD%A3%E5%BC%8F%E7%89%88%E4%B8%8B%E8%BC%89%E9%BB%9E

2)https://docs.google.com/open?id=0B1_STgPQEMn4QUxpeW9NNU5Ldnc

After you use Photocap software to generate the photo file formatted for a VISA photo, you can use a kiosk to print it out. I suggest selecting the 4x6 inch format to print it, as this would be much cheaper than using general photo stores. The following website link and Figure A-2 provide an example. You can use this solution to print your photo more affordably.

3)https://amingo6262.pixnet.net/blog/post/468552506

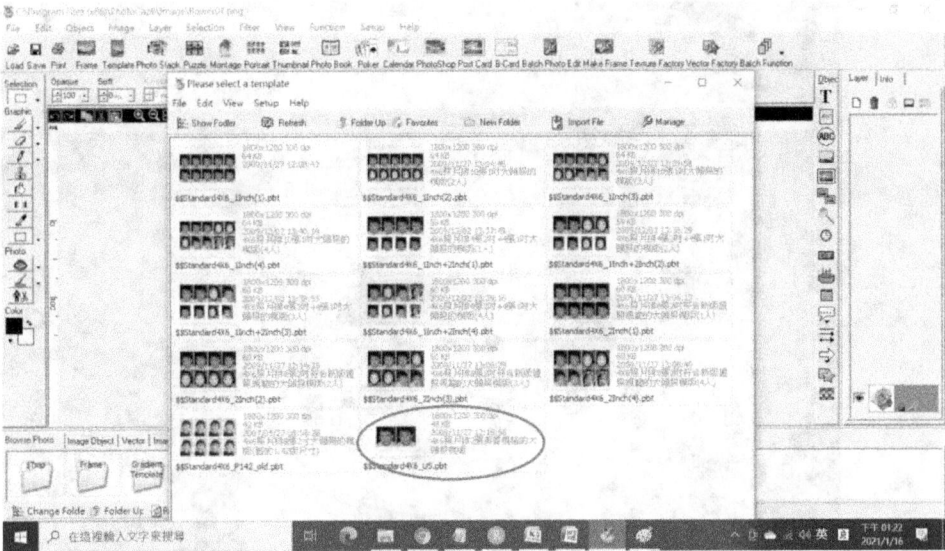

Figure A-1 The Free Photocap Software

Figure A-2 The Kiosk to Print Photo

References

American Institute in Taiwan, (2021), https://www.ait.org.tw/zhtw.

DS-260 Form example, (2021),
 https://travel.state.gov/content/dam/visas/DS-260-Exemplar.pdf

Google Scholar, (2021), http://scholar.google.com.

Google Patent, (2021), http://www.google.com/patents

Green Card Wikipedia, (2021), https://en.wikipedia.org/wiki/Green_card.

National Visa Center, (2021), https://travel.state.gov/content/travel/en/us-visas/immigrate/national-visa-center.html

Passport Photo Format, (2021) https://travel.state.gov/content/travel/en/us-visas/visa-information-resources/photos/photo-examples.html.

Police Certificate in U.K., (2021), https://www.acro.police.uk/police_certificates.aspx.

USCIS (United States Citizenship and Immigration Services),(2021), https://www.uscis.gov.

Unlock the Path to Your EB2/NIW Green Card—On a Budget, Even If You're Applying from Abroad Without an Employer!

Are you dreaming of obtaining permanent residency in the United States without breaking the bank? This book is your step-by-step guide to navigating the EB2/NIW (Employment-Based Second Preference with National Interest Waiver) green card process. Designed for individuals with advanced degrees or exceptional abilities, this visa category does not require a U.S. employer sponsor, making it accessible for many.

Author shares personal experiences of successfully applying for the EB2/NIW green card from abroad, offering invaluable insights and practical tips for every stage of the journey. Learn how to:

- Identify affordable legal assistance or go the DIY route.
- Prepare compelling reference and petition letters.
- Organize and submit supporting documents effectively.
- Navigate the DS-260, health exams, and interview process with confidence.
- Save money without compromising the quality of your application.

With meticulous advice, real-world examples, and a faith-based perspective, this book is a must-read for anyone seeking a streamlined and successful path to U.S. permanent residency.